## About the author

TOBY SHELLEY has reported from many countries in the Middle East, North Africa and sub-Saharan Africa over the course of twenty years as a journalist. He works for the *Financial Times*. Previously he was regional energy news editor for Dow Jones Newswires. He has covered many OPEC conferences and reported extensively on the oil industry in the North Sea. He contributes regularly to *Middle East International*. His most recent book is *Endgame in the Western Sahara: What Future for Africa's Last Colony?* (Zed Books, 2004).

# OIL

*Politics, Poverty and the Planet*

_____

**Toby Shelley**

University Press
*Dhaka*

White Lotus
*Bangkok*

Fernwood Publishing
*Nova Scotia*

Books for Change
*Bangalore*

World Book Publishing
*Beirut*

SIRD
*Kuala Lumpur*

TWN
*Penang*

David Philip
*Cape Town*

ZED BOOKS
*London & New York*

*Oil: Politics, Poverty and the Planet* was first published in 2005 by

**In Bangladesh**: The University Press Ltd,
Red Crescent Building, 114 Motijheel C/A, PO Box 2611, Dhaka 1000

**In Burma, Cambodia, Laos, Thailand and Vietnam**:
White Lotus Co. Ltd, GPO Box 1141, Bangkok 10501, Thailand

**In Canada**: Fernwood Publishing Ltd,
8422 St Margaret's Bay Road (Hwy 3) Site 2A, Box 5,
Black Point, Nova Scotia, BOJ 1BO

**In India**: Books for Change,
139 Richmond Road, Bangalore 560 025

**In Lebanon, Bahrain, Egypt, Jordan, Kuwait, Qatar, Saudi Arabia
and United Arab Emirates:** World Book Publishing, 282 Emile Eddeh
Street, Ben Salem bldg, PO Box 3176, Beirut, Lebanon www.wbpbooks.com

**In Malaysia**: Strategic Information Research Development (SIRD),
No. 11/4E, Petaling Jaya, 46200 Selangor

**In Southern Africa**: David Philip (an imprint of New Africa Books),
99 Garfield Road, Claremont 7700, South Africa

**In the rest of the world**: Zed Books Ltd, 7 Cynthia Street, London N1 9JF,
UK, and Room 400, 175 Fifth Avenue, New York, NY 10010, USA
www.zedbooks.co.uk

Copyright © Toby Shelley 2005

Designed and typeset in Monotype Bembo by Illuminati, Grosmont
Cover designed by Andrew Corbett
Printed and bound in the EU by Cox & Wyman, Reading

Distributed in the USA exclusively by Palgrave Macmillan, a division of
St Martin's Press, LLC, 175 Fifth Avenue, New York, NY 10010

A catalogue record for this book is available from the British Library
Library of Congress Cataloging-in-Publication Data available
Canadian CIP data is available from the National Library of Canada

ISBN 1 55266 165 2 Pb (Canada)
ISBN 9953 14 072 3 Pb (Lebanon)


ISBN 1 84277 520 0 Hb (Zed Books)
ISBN 1 84277 521 9 Pb (Zed Books)

# Contents

# List of tables

# INTRODUCTION

## Oil and natural gas: the issues

Energy is the precursor of economies. Its supply and utilisation underlie modes of production and social organisation. The source and availability of energy determine industrial development, means of transportation and subsistence. Shifting from non-traded forms of energy – gathered wood and biomass – on which billions of people still depend to coal to oil and natural gas has fundamentally changed social relations within and between regions of the world. The Middle East and Central Asia would not be in the eye of the global politico-military storm if they did not possess vast reserves of oil and natural gas. Right-wing lobbyists would not be championing an assertion of US hegemony in West Africa were it not for the uncovering of that region's deep-water oil and natural gas since the 1990s. Should there ever be a quantum shift from hydrocarbon dependence to other forms of energy supply, the economic and strategic implications would doubtless be as profound as those that accompanied the transition from coal to oil by the industrialised nations early in the last century.

This book has two aims. The first is simply to provide the reader with a digest of the information needed to understand the global structure of the oil and natural gas economy. There is data on where reserves lie, who produces what, trade patterns, consumption and prices. Drawing on studies by international bodies, the book picks out trends and forecasts for the coming two or three decades, including the growing importance of China.

The second aim, in the spirit of the Global Issues series, is to highlight vital political and social issues inherent in a global energy sector in which consumption remains dominated by the wealthy, post-colonial powers and export production by developing countries. It looks at the impact of dependence on hydrocarbon exports on the producer countries, finding not bloated, super-rich sheikhdoms of tabloid fantasy but economies deformed and made prone to civil strife by their reliance on commodities with the most volatile of prices. The distribution of earnings enriches the classes or cliques or families who control it while impoverishing the rest, and the scramble for control of oil wealth proves to be a major spur to conflict within countries and a source of tension between countries.

Another major area of discussion in this book is the inseparability of oil and natural gas supply security from the geostrategy of the powerful consumer countries of the OECD, particularly the US. In these countries little is heard of the cost of oil dependency for producer countries, but, should prices rise, the horrors of reliance on 'greedy', 'untrustworthy' foreigners are soon dragged to the fore by demagogues. Controlling access to hydrocarbon reserves has been an abiding feature of foreign policy since the First World War. It runs through the Cold War, the years of anti-colonial nationalism, the so-called War on Terror, and is already featuring in the shaping of future relations with China and Russia.

There is no serious doubt about the reality or the gravity of the environmental damage caused by fossil fuels. Among the questions that remain are how serious and how rapid the impact will be – which disease vectors will shift, which countries will first suffer massive flooding from sea level rise, what the response to mass migration from dessicated lands in the south will be. Mitigation of the problem poses other questions. For the bean counters in treasuries and expediency-minded politicians there is the question whether expenditure on the abatement of greenhouse gas emissions squares with the usual practice of going into an election promising lower taxes.

Energy demand is on a strong upward trend. Much is generated by the orgy of consumerism prevalent in wealthy countries. But demand growth is increasingly powered by the larger developing economies as they extend provision of electricity, gas for cooking and motorised transport to their own populations and as their industrial production ramps up, largely to feed exports to OECD countries whose corporations seek cheaper labour and less regulation of manufacturing. Should developing countries be forced to limit their growth or, with lesser financial resources, mitigate their pollution to bail the world out of a still deeper environmental catastrophe than that created over the last three centuries, for the most part by Europe and North America?

There is much talk of alternative energy sources. But often this is not for reasons of the environment but to ensure control over supply, so use of coal tar sands and solar power can sit side by side when the one deepens hydrocarbon dependency and the other reduces it. Looking at energy alternatives beneficial to the battle against greenhouse gas emissions, it is clear that a hydrocarbon-free future is a very long way off. With present technology the much-vaunted hydrogen economy would be based on oil, natural gas and coal. The issue of how to cope with our ever-growing thirst for oil and natural gas cannot be ducked. Precedent shows lower demand and greater efficiency to have been driven by high prices, not by worthy resolutions at international conferences.

It is worth noting what this book does not address. It does not deal in any detail with how energy is traded – the intricacies of term contracts and liftings, spot deals, futures and forwards and contracts for difference. Nor does it deal with the downstream oil industry – refining, petrochemicals, marketing – even though this has grown in importance in determining relations between particular producer countries and between particular producers and consumers. It is also not a book about the major oil companies, whose histories have been excellently covered elsewhere.

There are few if any answers in this book. That was not the intention. Lots of issues are raised and the reader must construct his or her own responses to the political, economic and environmental conditions created and reinforced by our oil- and natural-gas-based economies.

# I

# Insatiable demand and
# the quest for supply

Oil and natural gas are largely exports of the developing world, processed and consumed in the industrialised world. This they share with a host of commodities – metals from iron ore to the platinum group, minerals such as phosphate or titanium dioxide, as well as cotton, rubber, coffee and cocoa. Of the top ten oil consumers in 2002, six were members of the Organisation of Economic Cooperation and Development; so were seven of the top importers. By contrast, only two of the top ten exporters (but five of the top ten producers) were members of the industrialised countries' club.[1]

Yet where the dependence of producer countries on most commodities has either been limited or has declined, the dependence of major developing-country oil exporters on that one resource remains extraordinarily high. Where natural gas is associated with oil, coming from the same geological conditions, its rapid development as a fuel of choice will replicate this situation.

So, for Saudi Arabia, oil accounted for over 99 per cent of export income in 1977[2] and 94 per cent in 2002, even after decades of talk about and investment in economic diversification.

For Nigeria, once a major source of tropical commodities, oil accounted for over 93 per cent of export value in 1977 and 99 per cent in 2002. In Venezuela, which adopted the Mexican policy of 'sowing the oil' to expand away from total reliance on oil exports, there was some lessening, from around 95 per cent in 1977 to 75 per cent in 2002.

Algeria, where governments have long known the ratio of reserves to population to be more severe than for the Arab countries of the Gulf, and where oil was viewed through the 1960s and 1970s as the tool with which a Japan of the Maghreb would be built, oil's share of export value fell from 95 per cent in 1977 to under 70 per cent in 2002. However, in the intervening years Algeria had become a major exporter of natural gas, reinforcing its dependence on hydrocarbons. Qatar and Iran are two more major oil producers where natural gas (in its liquefied form) is set to emphasise the role of provider of energy for other economies. Indonesia, one of the countries most successful in managing its oil revenues during the price booms of the 1970s, is, ironically, the current member of the Organisation of Petroleum Exporting Countries by far and away the least dependent on oil. There oil now accounts for just 15 per cent of export value as reserves deplete.

For all of the international concern over global warming, the recurrent and geopolitically driven scares in the major consumer countries over security of supply, and the promises of new technology, the demand that created oil-based economies is projected to grow. And although oil and natural gas are indeed finite resources, there is no looming shortage of either. Indeed, while oil and gas will be sourced from an increasing number of countries, likely leading them into traps their predecessors fell into, the next two or three decades will only emphasise the dependence of the industrialised world on those former colonies, dependencies and mandate territories that sit on top of the bulk of the world's oil and natural gas. That said, with the rise of China as a manufacturing giant and India as an economic power, the profile of consumption will change. The trade in oil and natural gas will become more extensive and more complex.

## Feeding frenzy

Demand for oil in 2000 was some 75 million barrels a day, compared with less than 47 million in 1970 and 66 million in 1990. The reference case presented by the International Energy Agency (of which more later) posits a rise to 120 million barrels a day by 2030.[3] Another leading source of data, the US government's Energy Information Administration, confirms the trend. Its study of US energy to 2025 assumes world oil demand of over 123 million barrels a day by the end of the period.[4] Demand for natural gas is seen by the IEA as rising from some 2.5 trillion cubic metres to over 5 trillion by 2030. These two growth patterns can be combined by converting barrels a day and cubic metres a year into the common measure of tonnes of oil equivalent. Using that yardstick, the IEA calculates annual oil and natural gas consumption in 1971 to have been something under 3.35 billion tonnes of oil equivalent, rising to 5.69 billion in 2000 and projected to rise to not far short of 10 billion by 2030. The combined share of oil and gas in total energy supply was 69 per cent in 1971 and 62 per cent in 2000 (after the growth of nuclear and, to a much lesser extent, non-hydro renewable power). According to the reference case presented, by 2030, the proportion will be 66 per cent.[5] (These figures exclude use of biomass fuels such as wood in non-OECD countries.) So much for alternative sources of energy, to date.

Industrialised countries of the OECD currently account for over 60 per cent of world oil demand and 55 per cent of natural gas demand. The IEA reference case sees that dropping to 50 per cent and 48.5 per cent by 2030. OECD demand growth will average 0.8 per cent a year to 2030. For natural gas it will be over 2 per cent.

As a country the United States is far and away the biggest consumer of oil. In 2001, the US consumed 19.8 million barrels a day. Government calculations see that increasing to between 26.9 and 31.8 million barrels a day in 2025, depending on price and rate of economic growth. Given the size of the US in territorial, economic and demographic terms, it makes sense to compare its demand to that of the European Union and Pacific members of the OECD (Japan, Korea, Australia and New Zealand) rather than individual countries. The IEA put current EU members' oil consumption at 12.3 million barrels a day in 2000, rising to 13.9 million in 2030. For Pacific members of the OECD consumption in 2000 was 8.5 million barrels a day, rising to an assumed 10.5 million in 2030. US demand growth rates, according to these figures, remain higher than for the EU and OECD Pacific. The story is broadly the same for natural gas.

Consumption on this scale requires massive and increasing imports. The dependence of OECD economies on imports is growing, not only because of rising demand but also because of the depletion of domestic reserves in the traditional US onshore oil-producing states and the UK sector of the North Sea. Even by the early 1970s, the US had lost the ability to act as a 'swing producer' – one that can increase or decrease production in order to fill the requisite supply shortage. Net imports of 318,000 barrels a day in 1949 had multiplied tenfold by 1970, topped 7 million in 1976 and exceeded 10 million barrels a day – some one-eighth of world production – in 2000–2002. The UK North Sea, which came on stream in the mid-1970s, is now being abandoned slowly but surely by the big companies, and a decade after the 'dash for gas' the UK has been transformed from a natural gas exporter to a country with a deficit that could endanger power supplies in the case of an exceptionally cold winter.

US dependence on oil imports was around 20 per cent in the 1960s.[6] Under the five scenarios used by government, by 2025 it would be between 64.5 and 70 per cent,[7] with the actual volume of imports ranging from 17.8 to 22.2 million barrels a day. Japan and South Korea rank two and four in the list of major importers. Neither is a substantial oil producer, and the OECD Pacific set to which they belong already imports some 90 per cent of its oil. That will edge even higher in coming years. OECD Europe, which includes four of the top ten importers – Germany, France, Italy and Spain – will see dependence grow from some 50 per cent now to over 80 per cent in 2030, according to the IEA reference case.[8]

The same study projects OECD North America's dependence on imports of natural gas rising to 26 per cent in 2030 from just 1 per cent in 2000. In 2003 there were five liquefied natural gas import terminals in the US; industry estimates put the number of newbuilds proposed at thirty. For OECD Europe import dependence is seen as growing to 69 per cent from 36 per cent, while for OECD Pacific it declines to 50 per cent from a current 67 per cent.[9]

The consumption and importing of oil and natural gas has been dominated by the rich industrialised countries of the North and this remains the case overall. However, a major new player burst onto the stage when China became a net oil importer in the mid-1990s. Since then, the manufacturing boom there has powered demand for oil and gas. By 2002 China shared with Japan the number two slot in the rankings of top oil consumers at 5.3 million barrels a day and was the fifth biggest importer at 1.9 million barrels a day.[10] In July 2003, Chinese demand hit a record level of 5.59 million barrels a day, a staggering rise of over 19 per cent year-on-year, while the country's demand growth outstripped that of the US for the previous three years and total demand, set to outstrip Japan in 2003, was projected at 10.9 million barrels a day by 2025.[11] Dependence on imports is projected to rise from under 40 per cent now to 80 per cent in coming decades, ensuring that China will be increasingly important on the international oil markets. Natural gas usage in China is currently low and even by 2030 is projected by the IEA to be 162 billion cubic metres a year, of which around 30 per cent would be imported.

India is also already an important consumer and importer of oil, accounting for 2.1 million barrels a day in 2002, of which 1.4 million barrels a day were imported.[12] An annual growth rate of 3.3 per cent, taking 2030 consumption to 5.6 million barrels a day under the IEA reference case, would make India too a major market player.

## Production now and for the future

In 2002, the world's top ten oil producers included just three members of OPEC while five were members of the OECD – the US, Mexico, Norway, Canada and Britain. The top producer, at over 9 million barrels a day, was the US. OPEC linchpin Saudi Arabia held second place with some 8.5 million barrels a day of production. The other OPEC members were Iran and Venezuela, either side of 3 million barrels a day. At first glance this seems counter-intuitive and even a contradiction of the statement that oil and natural gas flow primarily from developing countries to industrialised countries. But the oil export rankings show the underlying picture. There, seven of the top ten are OPEC members (Saudi Arabia, Venezuela, Iran, the United Arab Emirates, Nigeria, Kuwait and Iraq), the other three being Russia, Norway and Mexico. The same is true of natural gas, where statistics show the US to be the second largest producer at 548 billion cubic metres a year, behind the Russian Federation at 555 billion.[13] Canada and the UK, too, are major producers, well ahead of anywhere in the Middle East and even of natural-gas-rich Algeria. However, the US has a natural gas deficit, which is currently plugged by pipeline imports from Canada but will be increasingly filled by liquefied natural gas (LNG) imports from developing countries in the Atlantic Basin. BG Group, the UK natural-gas producer, expects trading in the Atlantic Basin to see 24 per cent faster growth than the rest of the world after 2010 as West Africa, Egypt, Trinidad and Algeria boost exports to an increasingly gas-deficient US and Western Europe. It sees US demand for LNG growing by 28 per cent in 2003–08, against global LNG demand growth of 10 per cent.[14] The IEA's trade flow projections for 2030 tell a similar story.

So, consumption of oil and natural gas is set to continue its growth, and the import dependence of long-established and more recent major consumers will deepen. Who can meet the new demand? The answer depends on two factors: proven reserves and investment. Both are variables.

The rate of replacement of reserves is a key indicator of the performance of an oil company. The share price of Shell dived and senior executives lost their jobs when the group had to downgrade its reserve estimates in early 2004. Reserve replacement indicates the company's future production profile. For a country or a region, it determines the lifetime of the income stream from hydrocarbons and the degree of investor interest. In 2003, some

27 per cent of oil produced was from fields that were in decline and some 1 million barrels a day of new production were needed in order to replace depleted reserves. The forecast was for some eighteen large-scale projects producing up to 3 million barrels a day to come on stream in 2005 as recently found reserves were exploited, on top of 2 million barrels a day in 2004.[15]

OPEC's definition of proven reserves runs to twenty lines, but the crucial part reads:

> Proven reserves: an estimated quantity of all hydrocarbons statistically defined as crude oil or natural gas, which geological and engineering data demonstrate with reasonable certainty to be recoverable in future years from known reservoirs under existing economic and operating conditions.

To tease that out a bit, it is plain that if no exploration work has been done somewhere, no reserves will have been found, let alone proven. So Mauritania, for example, went through the 1990s with no proven reserves yet will become an oil-producing country in 2005–06 because oil companies discovered previously unfound oil and gas reservoirs.

The decision to explore in deep water and then to develop finds is driven by technical and market-related factors. Deep-water exploration and production techniques pioneered in the North Sea and the Gulf of Mexico have now become generalised and less prohibitively expensive, so consortia of small and medium-sized companies are able to undertake projects like those offshore Mauritania.[16] The global forecast is for some $56 billion to be spent on deep-water oil projects between 2003 and 2008, with output rising from 2.4 million barrels a day in 2002 to over 8 million barrels a day well before 2020, due to 'gamechanger' technological developments.[17] But whether it is worthwhile exploring or producing depends on the cost of finding and producing each barrel of oil or cubic metre of natural gas, compared to prevailing and forecast prices at which they can be sold. The oil industry's confidence in the production-cost to sale-price ratio is reflected in the utilisation of drilling rigs, and there are industry indexes that record this. Definitions of proven reserves change, then, according to commercial and technical factors. And some of those are driven by political considerations – whether consumer countries are willing to buy from certain producers. In the 1960s the US persuaded NATO members to eschew long-term or large-scale oil-purchase deals with the Soviet Union. Since the collapse of the Soviet Union, Russian oil and gas reserves have become the Holy Grail of Western oil companies; major Russian oil corporations have developed; enormous funds are being poured into multiphase projects, notably that at Sakhalin in the Russian Far East. Far from discouraging imports of Russian oil, Washington has encouraged them, while Western Europe clamours for Russian natural gas. The proven oil reserves of the former Soviet Union were upgraded by 19 per cent between 2001 and 2002.

In the ten years 1993–2002, proven oil reserves of the Middle East rose some 5 per cent to 699 billion barrels, those of Africa rose over 45 per cent to some 94 billion, and those of the former Soviet Union increased over 35 per cent to some 78 billion. Latin America's proven reserves ended the decade at 111 billion barrels, a slide of around 15 per cent. On these figures, the Middle East accounts for some 65 per cent of global proven oil reserves. Middle East members of OPEC account for over 55 per cent. Meanwhile, the shares of North America, Asia–Pacific and Western Europe have been falling. In the UK North Sea there is an ongoing process of withdrawal by the oil giants Shell and BP as remaining reserves become too management-intensive for corporations looking to exploit far bigger fields. This process has spawned a generation of small, independent oil companies, known as 'scavengers', who buy up assets from the majors and produce from them more cheaply. The process is expected to be repeated in Norway.

The Middle East's centrality as a repository of natural gas is not quite as striking, accounting for 40 per cent of the world total in 2002, but it is again the dominant region, with the former Soviet Union taking second place with 32 per cent and Asia–Pacific and Africa coming in with well under 10 per cent each. Between them, Western Europe and North America account for another 8 per cent or so.[18]

The IEA is clear in its *World Energy Outlook 2002*[19] that, while better technology may arrest the rate of long-term decline in North America and the North Sea, and Canada, Mexico and Norway may see short-term rises in oil production, the only non-OPEC producing countries that will register significant increases in oil production are Russia, Kazakhstan, Azerbaijan, Brazil and Angola. In the first three of these, prospects will be dependent on investment levels. In the latter two, the successful deployment of technology is also a key factor. Russian (as opposed to former Soviet Union) oil production – not exports – is assumed to rise to 8.6 million barrels a day by 2010, having notched up almost monthly records through the early years of this decade, reaching 9.5 million barrels a day by 2030.

Kazakhstan and Azerbaijan could reach a combined total of 3.5 million barrels a day by 2010 if investment is found. But that compares to 35.9 million barrels a day for OPEC, over 40 per cent of global supply. Almost 30 per cent of the global supply would be from OPEC's Middle East members. Under the same reference case, OPEC's share of the global market would rise from 38.4 per cent in 2000 to over 54 per cent in 2030, with Middle East members' share increasing faster than for the organisation as a whole. Concomitantly, non-OPEC and OECD shares fall. Some analysts believe the IEA overstates OPEC's dominance but only by a matter of degree – the trend is undisputed. Okugu, for example, posits OPEC as having a 40 per cent share of a 91 million barrel market by 2020.[20] A study for an OPEC publication suggested much higher Russian output of around 12 million barrels a day by 2010, which, if proposed export routes were developed, would translate into exports of over 7 million barrels a day by 2010.[21] As a former senior figure in OPEC told a London conference, 'This decade belongs to non-OPEC producers but the next decade belongs to OPEC.'

Trends in natural-gas supply are more dependent on proximity and investment than are oil supply trends. Natural gas cannot be simply pumped into a tanker or loaded onto a truck or rail wagon. It must be transported by pipeline or treated for sea shipment. The fast expanding method of shipment is in liquefied form. While costs of liquefaction and re-gasification are falling, the process remains capital intensive. Russia and other former Soviet Union states and the Middle East will be the principal exporters to Western Europe and the US. As a BG Group executive said, 'The Middle East will become the nexus of production going forward, with the Atlantic Basin at its heart.'

## Financing the consumption boom

The scale of investment required by the oil and natural gas industry is vast. The forecast capital expenditure of BP in 2003 was $14–14.5 billion, or more than the 1999 gross domestic product of each of 83 of the 162 countries surveyed in the UN Development Programme's 2001 Human Development Report. In 2003, Royal Dutch/Shell disposed of inadequately performing operations worth $4 billion. Phase II alone of Shell, Mitsui and Mitsubishi's Sakhalin oil and gas development in the far east of

Russia was costed at $10 billion, the biggest ever investment in Russia. In the Middle East, the Dolphin project to pipe natural gas from Qatar to Abu Dhabi, Dubai, Oman and then Pakistan was expected to cost $8–10 billion. The Saudi Gas Initiative that would have opened up Saudi Arabia's giant natural gas fields to foreign consortia comprising ExxonMobil, Shell, BP, Phillips Petroleum, Occidental Petroleum, Marathon Oil, TotalFinaElf and Conoco was costed at $25 billion. Even the relatively small Chinguetti development offshore Mauritania, which will produce some 75,000 barrels a day and make the country an oil exporter, will require capital expenditure of some $400 million, well in excess of the value of Mauritania's current total annual exports.

The long-term, global investment requirements for the energy sector as a whole – taking in electricity and coal as well as oil and natural gas – are vast. The IEA publishes every two years a *World Energy Investment Outlook*. The 2003 edition estimates that in the period 2001–30 some $16 trillion will have been needed to expand and replace capacity.[22] Although that amounts to only 1 per cent of estimated global GDP, the burden is greater for some regions – 4 per cent for Africa and 5 per cent for Russia.

It is in fact electricity that will take up 60 per cent of the investment. But oil and natural gas will require an average of $208 billion a year, over $6.1 trillion in total, with natural gas taking a little over half. Exploration and development will take up the lion's share of the total.

For oil, 69 per cent of total investment, under the IEA scenario, will be outside the OECD but largely geared towards supplying OECD countries. OECD investment is high relative to production capacity because of higher costs. Conversely, the Middle East's share of upstream spending is, at 20 per cent, low compared to its production and capacity because the costs of production, which give Middle East producers competitive advantage, are low.

Upstream OECD investment for the thirty-year period is put at $684 billion, with the Middle East requiring $408 billion, Russia $308 billion, Africa $311 billion, Latin America $241 billion, South and East Asia $87 billion and China $69 billion.

As with oil, some 40 per cent of total investment in natural gas in non-OECD countries will be geared towards exporting to OECD countries. For Russia the percentage is lower at 31 per cent because of proximity to markets and established infrastructure. However, for the Middle East it rises to 70 per cent and for Africa it is 65 per cent. Exploration and development plus LNG project investment spend in the industrialised countries outweighs that for the rest of the world at $928 billion, against $192 billion for Russia and between $140 billion and $168 billion for each of South and East Asia, Latin America, the Middle East and Africa.

Investment, like proven reserves, is a variable rather than a fixed factor. Banks are willing to lend and shareholders to invest on the basis of returns relative to other sectors or projects and on the basis of the security of their investment. The first of these variables depends in large part on the future price of oil and natural gas, just as oil companies' willingness to explore and develop does. After all, for BP in 2004, a $1 a barrel swing in the price of oil would affect annual pre-tax earnings by $570 million.[23]

In fact, despite the enormous volatility of the oil price (to which many gas prices are linked, directly or indirectly), which has swung from $10 a barrel to over $50 a barrel in the 1997–2004 period and may vary by several per cent on a single day, the return on oil and natural gas investment is healthy. For integrated oil and natural gas companies, those with upstream and downstream operations, the return on investment for 1993–2002 was the highest for any industry at some 12 per cent. For those with only exploration and production it was a lesser 7 per cent and for refiners and marketers over 9 per cent, compared with about 11 per cent for the retail industry, 9 per cent for machinery and computer makers, 8 per cent for primary metals and less for communications and for real estate.

On the slightly different yardstick of return on average capital employed, ExxonMobil, the world's biggest oil company, made a return of 17.8 per cent in 2001 and 13.5 per cent in 2002. Shell and BP both achieved a massive 19 per cent in 2001, falling to 14 per cent and 13 per cent, respectively, the following year. That was across all operations. Exploration and production, though, remain the core of the companies and the most profitable part, with Shell's upstream businesses achieving a return of 28 per cent in 2002 on the back of high oil prices, against 26.8 per cent for Exxon. BP targeted a rise in its overall return of 3 percentage points by 2006 as it focused on five profit centres it viewed as particularly attractive – Angola, Azerbaijan, Trinidad, Gulf of Mexico and Asia–Pacific LNG.[24]

Yet political and economic risks are factored into investment decisions, and these can seriously blunt the appetite of potential investors. The nationalisation of BP's assets in Nigeria in 1979, the war in Angola, and civil conflict along the west coast of Africa created a perception of risk that put off some oil companies and investors, although the chief executive of an independent oil company long active in West Africa said he could think of no example of a government seizing oil company assets since the Nigerian case. In Angola and Algeria, both subject to long-running and bloody strife, the oil and natural gas industries have largely been insulated from the conflict. In part this has been because of the geographical isolation of production but in large part it has also been because groups contesting power have known that they too would need hydrocarbon income to sustain their rule.

The Canadian company Petrokazakhstan decided to list its shares in London because its board believed there was an understanding of emerging markets and attendant risks there that could not be found in New York or Toronto.

Of course, there are risks in investing in many oil- and natural-gas-producing countries. Smaller Western oil companies have complained they are discriminated against in Russian courts and subject to pressures that sometimes seem intended to drive them away from projects, leaving the way for Russian companies to move in. When BP announced it was to invest $6.8 billion in a joint venture with TNK of Russia in 2003 the move was greeted as a bill of good health for Russia. Just months later the arrest of oil oligarch Mikhail Khodorkovsky and comments from the defence minister about the need to retain control over strategic sectors of the economy resurrected fears of a move towards a Chinese style of economic and political development rather than an echo of European or North American capitalism.

The chronic instability of the Middle East, deriving from the occupation of Palestine and expressed in the prevalence of regimes with different political antecedents but a common predeliction for authoritarian rule, casts a shadow over the world's most prolific exporting region. The IEA refers to

> a backdrop of continuing political instability in the region. The US-led occupation of Iraq, endless and exhausting negotiations over a peace deal between Israel and Palestine, the social and political tensions throughout compound the political and economic unpredictability of the region.[25]

More specific investment uncertainties include access to reserves. The major Gulf producers nationalised upstream operations in the 1970s. Moves to reintroduce foreign oil companies have proved politically sensitive, generating in Kuwait, for example, parliamentary questioning of a perceived loss of sovereignty over resources, in Saudi Arabia reports of serious disagreement within the regime, and in Iran arguments about how deals could be structured to be acceptable to religious leaders. Middle Eastern governments have also tended to stand their ground in commercial negotiations, which in the case of Iran have dragged on for years.

Domestic investment in the oil and natural gas industries is constrained by lack of domestic lending capacity and by state control of national oil companies, according to the IEA. The upper limit of domestic bank lending for energy projects is around $600 million for Saudi Arabia, inadequate to fund necessary future developments. At the same time, the government's overall budgetary requirements can limit the capital left for investment – at $20 a barrel average for 2003, the deficit was set to exceed $10 billion but at $25 a barrel it would be balanced. With the price surge of 2004, a surplus of $30 billion was forecast.

Strategic decision-making by large OPEC producers represents another key variable. Individually and collectively the large-reserve, low-cost members keep a wary eye on the impact of the oil price and policy of other producers. High oil prices encourage production from higher-cost regions, eroding the market share of low-cost producers. So, there is always the temptation to increase production in an attempt to regain market share at a lower price that will squeeze out competitors. The calculations of gains and losses over different periods of time are a major factor in the policymaking of individual countries and groups of countries. A decision to restrain output and drive up prices may imply a lower investment spend, whereas a strategic decision by one or more major producers to pursue market share implies an expansion of capacity and hence of investment spend.

The IEA believes there is 'a real risk that production capacities in the region will not be developed as quickly as expected in the Reference Scenario. Under a low Middle East investment scenario, oil prices rise and so pare demand rises. However, the agency calculates that for OPEC members as a whole and for Middle

East members in particular, higher prices would not compensate for lower market share. Rather, non-OPEC African producers and Russia would reap the benefits.

The investment outlook for natural gas is more acute, the IEA believes. The longer supply chains in trade of natural gas, changing market structures and pricing mechanisms all introduce uncertainties, as do the cost, scale and complexity of developments that will increasingly limit financing and execution to the very largest companies or consortia. As consumer countries source natural gas from further afield, country risk becomes a bigger factor in investment decisions. Long-distance export pipelines concatenate political risk the more borders they cross: 'Geopolitical factors are especially important to the prospects for developing long distance pipelines in the Middle East and Central Asia.'[26] Russia's status as a 'transition economy' is underlined by the uncertainty that remains over long-term tax and legislative issues. For example, there are fears the natural gas behemoth Gazprom could be a milk cow for government, limiting its ability to invest. Then there have been legislative changes to the framework for foreign company participation in projects. Apparent disjuncture between local, regional and federal government policy adds to uncertainty.

So, the evidence is clear. Demand for oil and natural gas remains on an upward trend. To be sure, in the economic uncertainty of 2002 it dipped but by 2003 it had resumed firm growth, with 2004 demand growth particularly strong and 2005 forecasts robust. Longer-term outlooks pencil in burgeoning consumption out to 2025 and 2030. Consumption has long been led by the old industrialised powers but major developing countries are increasingly leading growth, in part as their own ability to consume grows but in large measure because faster and cheaper transport means their low-cost labour can be exploited by Western manufacturers. In its first forecast for 2005, the IEA reckoned OECD demand growth would be under 1 per cent while for China it would be over 8 per cent.[27]

Notwithstanding the huge oil and natural gas production of the US and the sizeable if relatively short-run output of the North Sea, the thirst for hydrocarbons from the OECD countries means oil and natural gas trade is primarily a transfer of resources from developing countries to developed. The Soviet Union, which fell into neither category, was relatively insulated from global trading for much of its history. Despite the scare stories that appear every few years, there is plenty of oil and gas left in the ground. Current reserves will satisfy demand for over four decades, according to BP's 2004 outlook and, as will be seen later, those reserve numbers do not take into account the potential offered by alternative ways of accessing suitable molecules.

The location of reserves of hydrocarbons in the developing world and the demand profiles of the OECD countries ensure that relationship will continue. But it is being altered by the economic growth of developing countries with a hydrocarbon deficit like China and India, increasingly important players in the oil market. The impact of the so-called transitional economies of the former Soviet Union also changes the picture somewhat — while the Central Asian states are developing countries in all but taxonomy, Russia cannot be so classified although its future as an archetypal capitalist economy of the OECD is far from assured.

Even if more oil and natural gas are sourced from Russia and even if consumer countries scout further and further afield with more and more advanced technology, the ongoing preponderance of traditional oil-exporting regions is not questioned. The role of the member countries of OPEC will increase. What is less certain is whether despite a tightness of production capacity that became evident in 2004, financing will be put in place to match demand growth.

**Table 1**   World oil and natural gas proven reserves, 2002

| Region | Oil (million barrels) | Gas (billion standard cubic metres) |
|---|---|---|
| North America | 27,646.0 | 6898.3 |
| of which US | 22,446.0 | 5,195.7 |
| Latin America | 111,172.7 | 7,507.4 |
| Eastern Europe | 79,190.5 | 57,492.8 |
| of which former USSR | 77,832.0 | 56,943.6 |
| Western Europe | 18,268.5 | 6,954.6 |
| Middle East | 698,906.3 | 71,546.0 |
| Africa | 93,549.5 | 13,207.1 |
| Asia Pacific | 38,434.0 | 14,118.0 |
| **Total** | **1,067,167.4** | **177,724.2** |
| of which OPEC | 847,718.8 | 86,828.0 |
| OPEC as % of total | 79.4 | 48.9 |

*Source*: OPEC.

**Table 2**   Top ten oil producers, 2003

| Country | Oil production (million barrels/day) |
|---|---|
| Saudi Arabia | 9.95 |
| United States | 8.84 |
| Russia | 8.44 |
| Iran | 3.87 |
| Mexico | 3.79 |
| China | 3.54 |
| Norway | 3.27 |
| Canada | 2.66 |
| United Arab Emirates | 2.66 |
| Venezuela | 2.58 |

*Source*: EIA.

**Table 3**  Top ten gas producers, 2003

| Country | Gas production (million tonnes of oil equivalent/year) |
| --- | --- |
| United States | 490.8 |
| Russia | 520.8 |
| UK | 92.5 |
| Algeria | 74.5 |
| Iran | 71.1 |
| Norway | 66.0 |
| Indonesia | 65.3 |
| Saudi Arabia | 54.9 |
| United Arab Emirates | 40.0 |
| Mexico | 32.7 |

*Source*: BP.

**Table 4**  Global oil demand

| Region | Production (million barrels/day) | | | |
| --- | --- | --- | --- | --- |
| | 2000 | 2010 | 2020 | 2030 |
| OECD North America | 22.2 | 24.8 | 27.7 | 30.8 |
| OECD Europe | 14.1 | 15.3 | 16.0 | 16.4 |
| OECD Pacific | 8.5 | 9.5 | 10.3 | 10.5 |
| OECD total | 44.8 | 49.6 | 54.0 | 57.6 |
| Russia | 2.7 | 3.1 | 3.7 | 4.4 |
| China | 4.9 | 7.0 | 9.4 | 12.0 |
| India | 2.1 | 3.0 | 4.2 | 5.6 |
| Other non-OECD | 11.8 | 22.8 | 28.9 | 36.3 |
| Non-OECD total | 27.1 | 35.9 | 46.4 | 58.3 |
| **Grand total** | **75.0** | **88.8** | **104.0** | **120.0** |
| Range of alternative estimates of grand total | – | 83–90 | 89–107 | – |

*Source*: IEA, CGES, EIA, OPEC.

**Table 5**  World natural gas demand

| Region/grouping | Demand (billion cubic metres) | | | |
| --- | --- | --- | --- | --- |
| | 2000 | 2010 | 2020 | 2030 |
| OECD | 1,392 | 1,800 | 2,161 | 2,449 |
| Transition economies (including former USSR) | 609 | 748 | 876 | 945 |
| Asia | 166 | 296 | 462 | 615 |
| Latin America | 105 | 167 | 251 | 373 |
| Middle East | 201 | 272 | 349 | 427 |
| Africa | 53 | 95 | 155 | 239 |
| World | 2,527 | 3,377 | 4,254 | 5,047 |

*Source*: IEA.

**Table 6**  Nominal and real oil prices (basis 1973)

| Year | Nominal oil price (US$/barrel) | Oil price adjusted for exchange rates and inflation (US$/barrel) |
| --- | --- | --- |
| 1973 | 3.05 | 3.05 |
| 1974 | 10.73 | 9.68 |
| 1979 | 17.25 | 9.04 |
| 1981 | 32.51 | 15.55 |
| 1982 | 32.38 | 15.93 |
| 1986 | 13.53 | 5.50 |
| 1990 | 22.26 | 6.38 |
| 1994 | 15.53 | 4.22 |
| 1998 | 12.28 | 3.19 |
| 2000 | 27.60 | 7.78 |
| 2002 | 24.36 | 6.55 |
| 2003 | 28.10 | 6.53 |

*Note*: Arabian Light official price to 1982; OPEC basket of crudes thereafter.
*Source*: OPEC.

**Table 7**   Oil and oil products as a proportion of export earnings of OPEC countries

| Year | Total exports (US$ billion) | Oil and oil products exports[*] (US$ billion) | Oil and oil products exports (as % of all exports) |
|------|------|------|------|
| 1977 | 149.2 | 141.6 | 95 |
| 1980 | 299.9 | 282.6 | 94 |
| 1986 | 98.7 | 76.0 | 77 |
| 1990 | 191.5 | 146.0 | 76 |
| 1995 | 207.9 | 133.5 | 64 |
| 1998 | 196.3 | 107.4 | 55 |
| 2000 | 347.2 | 249.6 | 72 |
| 2002 | 301.5 | 206.6 | 69 |

[*] Not including natural gas.

*Source*: OPEC.

# 2

# Conflict, poverty, inequality:
## the mixed blessing of oil

Oil and natural gas are valuable commodities in long-term demand but the income derived from their export is not an unalloyed blessing. Indeed, studies of the use of oil income are scattered with phrases such as 'the Dutch disease', 'the commodity curse' and, more colourfully, 'the Devil's excrement'.

This chapter looks at the economic, social and political impact of oil on producer countries. It examines how much income oil and gas generates, whether that income benefits the population at large, and whether the windfall earnings that states have accrued have transformed the economies or locked them into hydrocarbon dependency. It then touches on questions of sovereignty and regional stability presented by oil and gas wealth. The chapter moves on to consider instances where the oil industry has been a factor in domestic instability. It closes with the question of whether new oil and natural gas producers can avoid the pitfalls of their predecessors.

## The revenue roller-coaster

We have seen that major oil producers have had only limited success in diversifying their exports away from oil and oil products, which accounted for 94 per cent of Saudi Arabia's and 99 per cent of Nigeria's exports earnings in 2002. Some countries like Venezuela, Algeria and Iran have managed to reduce dependency, but the advent of large-scale natural gas exports in the last two cases is reproducing hydrocarbon dependency. Already more than half of Algeria's hydrocarbon income comes from gas and it aims to triple exports by 2010.[1] Even when economies have managed to diversify, the importance of oil to government revenues can linger. For example, oil export revenues have declined from 70 per cent of Mexican exports to just 7 per cent since the early 1980s but account for one-third of government income because the national oil company, Pemex, is state owned.[2] Russia is rarely thought of as an oil- and gas-dependent state. Yet oil and gas accounted for 20 per cent of GDP in 1999 and a quarter of federal revenues; as the country emerged from its economic crisis of 1998 it was growing oil sector revenues that accounted for 80 per cent of gains, which amounted to around 5 per cent of GDP.[3]

For oil-dependent states, of course, the whole economy and not just export earnings are strongly influenced by oil output and prices. In the last weeks of 1997, the Asian economic crisis struck and subsequent lack of demand for oil brought prices crashing to twelve-year lows in 1998. The value of oil exports of OPEC member countries plunged from some \$163 billion to \$107 billion. The fall in aggregate gross domestic product was 16 per cent, from some \$791 billion to under \$663 billion. By the same token, the partial recovery in prices in 1999 increased aggregate oil export earnings by around 45 per cent, while aggregate GDP grew well over 12 per cent. This volatility of export earnings is a constant feature of the oil producers. Looking back at earnings for the past twenty years, excluding the 'oil shocks' of 1973 and 1979 when prices rose sharply, the variation is considerable. From 1982 to 1986 earnings fell every year, starting at $204 billion and finishing at just $76 billion. They did not exceed the 1982 level until 2000. Earnings in 1990 were over a third higher than in 1989, due to the Iraqi invasion of Kuwait, but 1991 brought a 13 per cent drop and 1993 another fall of over 10 per cent. The same patterns are repeated broadly in the GDP figures.[4]

Forecasts for 2003 suggested that export earnings for Russia would rise 27 per cent, for Mexico 21 per cent, for Angola 16 per cent.[5] For OPEC members the forecast was for a 19 per cent rise, even taking into account the fall in Iraqi output due to the US-led invasion, a damaging strike in Venezuela early in the year and Indonesia's unremitting depletion of reserves.[6] The further price rises of 2004 promised greater gains, with some analysts raising medium-term price forecasts by several dollars a barrel.

The economic consequences of price volatility feed into the politics of producer countries. The worsening situation in Algeria in the late 1980s has been linked to the collapse in oil revenues as the price of crude and the value of the dollar fell.[7] The widespread protests of 1988 led, positively, to an end of one-party rule. But that was accompanied by a growth in political Islamism, which led to the annulment of elections and a decade of bloodletting. The rise in oil revenues in the early years of this decade, reaching $24 billion in 2003, enabled the Benflis government to announce a $10 billion package of public-sector-led expansion, a strategy some saw as repeating the errors of windfall utilisation of the past.

For good or ill, oil revenue windfalls can provide a cushion against the demands of international financial institutions. The Angolan government has been able to avoid both donor aid and structural adjustment prescriptions for much of its time in office.

Two staff-monitored International Monetary Fund programmes foundered, the second coming into being in the late 1990s after oil prices crashed and being abandoned as financial pressures eased with the recovery of prices in 2000–2001.[8]

Oil is traded in US dollars. This means that in addition to the impact of inflation on the purchasing power of oil revenues, there is the effect of the changing strength of the dollar on real income. Indeed, the ending of the Bretton Woods agreement was a major spur to OPEC members to begin to assert some control over oil prices. In 2003, the weakness of the dollar and consequent reduction of purchasing power were used to justify an OPEC decision not to increase output and so reduce dollar-denominated oil prices. In real terms, the price of oil peaked in 1982 at $15.93 a barrel (basis 1973). Its nadir since then was in 1998 when it was just $3.19, scarcely above the average level for 1973 before the full impact of the first price 'shock'. In 2002 it was $6.53, only two-thirds of the 1974 price.[9]

OPEC revenues, in real terms based on a year 2000 US dollar, peaked in 1980 at $598 billion, with the 1998 low point seeing them earning just $113 billion, lower even than for 1986, the year of the previous price collapse. For the 1990s net oil export revenues for OPEC countries were $1.6 trillion, less than half of the $3.3 trillion earned in the 1970s. The period 2001 to mid-2003 showed an improvement of around 20 per cent over 1990s earnings but this was still way below the 1970s and 1980s.[10]

## Smoothing the ride

So much for the income accruing to countries. Populations have grown since oil became a big earner for producing states. For the OPEC member countries, the population total rose from 296 million in 1977 to 532 million in 2002. There is evidence that oil income stimulated population growth. In the 1970s and 1980s the annual population growth rates for oil-producing countries in the Middle East and North Africa exceeded those of non-oil producers in the region by 2.5 percentage points.[11] Declining oil revenues and growing populations overlie the even more fundamental reality that oil and natural gas reserves are finite. This points up the policy choices posed by the revenue stream, which can be deployed for the long term through investment or burnt up in short-term consumption.

One policy option is the establishment of a fund to manage a portion of revenues. There are two distinct types of fund: the stabilisation fund that smooths the unevenness of revenues caused by the volatility of oil prices; and the savings fund, which is intended to pass on part of the revenue gain from finite reserves to future generations. An alternative to the stabilisation fund is hedging on the oil and natural gas derivatives markets – smoothing the revenue stream by 'locking in' a price range through contracts committing the government's agent and counterparty to exchange oil at a given price at a given time in the future. The seller loses out when prices on the spot market are higher than the agreed price, but wins when they are lower. Mexico has experimented with hedging. Kuwait runs both types of fund, and it was the finance from these that permitted the ruling family and its government to operate in exile after the Iraqi invasion of August 1990. Dipping into the savings fund had been forbidden, but a partial waiver was issued to fund reconstruction work in 1991.

The problem with either kind of fund is that the probity of its management is only as great as that of the institutions that oversee it. The stabilisation fund in Norway is frequently cited as a paradigm of transparency – all transfers in and out of the fund must be cleared through parliament. Transfers out of the fund must go through the budget to prevent the establishment of a parallel government financing system. When East Timor announced in 2003 that it planned a hybrid stabilisation and savings fund with assets invested abroad, it cited Norway as a model it hoped to improve on.[12]

The aspirations of the government in Dili stand in contrast to reports from Ashgabat, where the Turkmen president is reputed to have personal control over the Foreign Exchange Reserve Fund, which is fed by hydrocarbon and cotton revenues.

Despite the clear problems of ensuring transparency and accountability in countries where civil society and political opposition are not strong enough to ensure it, the international financial institutions have seen revenue management as a means of sanitising projects that might otherwise be difficult to approve.

The plan approved for Chad has been trumpeted by the companies and institutions concerned (and by some non-governmental organisations) as a model for the future. The massively controversial Chad–Cameroon oil pipeline will increase Chad's budget by 50 per cent, so introducing all of the perils of the windfall. The World Bank imposed as a condition of funding a revenue management plan with a nine-member oversight committee to approve expenditure. But, as a report comparing three countries' funds pointed out, four members are appointed by the president, two are from parliament, which is controlled by the president's political party, and one is from the government-overseen judiciary. Furthermore, although the fund's remit is to finance specified priority sectors such as health, education and water, with 10 per cent set aside for future generations, the law setting this out can be overturned after five years.[13]

However, there is another critique of the Chad plan:

> For the first time ever, an African nation has agreed to surrender part of its sovereignty over how to spend the money earned by a foreign company exploiting the country's oil reserves through pressure brought

about by the World Bank, the United States government and major oil companies, all acting in unison.

Under the new arrangement the American administration will in fact have de facto control over Chad's politics and finances.[14]

In Azerbaijan the State Oil Fund has been used to finance part of the government's investment in the proposed Baku–Ceyhan pipeline, another project that is being contested tooth and nail by a coalition of human rights and environmental non-governmental organisations. The fund is audited annually but there has been criticism that its oversight board is dominated by the government. The fund established for Kazakhstan has also been slated for excessive governmental control.

## Bitter harvest from 'sowing the oil'

The evidence is that oil-dependent states have been unable to convert oil revenues into sustainable economic growth. As Abed and Davoodi note,

> in the last 30 years, per capita income in the oil producing countries [of the Middle East and North Africa] declined at a rate of 1.3 per cent per annum, compared with an increase of 2 per cent per annum in the non-oil economies. Even during the booming 1970s, oil producing countries grew, in real per capita terms, at about half the rate of non-oil producing countries in the region.[15]

With developing countries as a whole, the comparison is even bleaker.

In the 1990s Sachs and Warner published an influential paper[16] demonstrating a negative correlation between a country's resource exports as a proportion of GDP and annual growth rates. The study controlled for a wide variety of other factors and looked at ninety-five countries over the period 1970–90. It also found that the negative relationship held during periods of booming commodity prices and slumping prices. Sachs and Warner then looked at a group of oil exporters and found the negative association to be even stronger than for all the commodity exporters studied. Indeed, in the periods for which data was available, the overall economies of Iraq, Kuwait, Qatar, Saudi Arabia and the UAE contracted.

What is remarkable looking at oil-producing countries is their diversity in terms of geography, demography and history. Yet, by and large, they share a failure to reap long-term economic growth from a valuable commodity for which demand is growing.

At the levels of rhetoric and policy announcement, regimes overseeing oil revenues in the 1970s and 1980s had targeted growth in the non-oil economy, diversification away from oil, and consolidation of national control over hydrocarbons. Abdelhamid Brahimi, former Algerian prime minister, depicts President Houari Boumedienne's economic policy as one of creating a North African manufacturer comparable to the economic 'miracle' of post-war Japan but one founded on oil.

In Venezuela and Mexico the slogan 'sowing the oil' was intended to lead to industrialisation and diversification. Terry Lynn Karl quotes Venezuelan president Carlos Andrés Pérez telling him 'Americans will be driving cars built by our workers in our modern factories, with bumpers made from our aluminium, and gasoline made from our oil. And we will look like you.'[17]

A drive towards import-substitution industries was encouraged, in part, by international institutions. The UN Commission for Latin America bought into the 'Prebisch hypothesis' that resource-based growth would be frustrated by a structural, long-term decline in commodity prices, the commission going on to recommend tariff-protected industrialisation.

The price increases of 1973–74 brought vast revenue increases to OPEC producers. Gelb's study of the impact of the use of the windfalls of 1973 and 1979 by six oil-producing countries details their failure to achieve economic transformation. The six (Algeria, Ecuador, Indonesia, Nigeria, Trinidad and Tobago, and Venezuela), reaped a windfall of $22.5 billion in 1974, averaging a massive 22.7 per cent of GDP. Only Indonesia, the least oil-dependent of the six, and possibly Ecuador achieved a strengthening of non-oil sectors in the period of the two price booms. Only these two saw agricultural and food production rise between 1974 and 1983,[18] and the overall non-oil economies of the six countries fell well below the norm for developing countries.

## Dutch disease and wasted windfalls

One explanation used by economists for the weakening of non-oil sectors of economies is the 'Dutch disease'. There are two competing accounts of the origin of the phrase. One is that it refers to the mutation of the Dutch economy during the tulip boom of the sixteenth century; the other is that it derives from the impact of natural gas development and export in the 1960s. The theory states that large windfalls in one sector tend to drive up the exchange rate, making exports of other sectors more expensive and imports cheaper. In the process, capital resources are drained from agriculture and manufacturing and sucked into services, transportation, construction and other non-tradable parts of the economy.

At the same time, while the funds accruing to government may boost the public sector and, in turn, translate into contracts for private-sector companies, the higher prices that have created a windfall for government may add to the cost base of the private sector. The oil windfall amounted to $51.5 billion between 1975 and 1981 for the Mexican public sector, but over the same period the private sector saw its income cut by $16 billion due to higher oil prices.[19]

Dependence on resources, it has also been argued, fails to build forward or backward linkages that stimulate other parts of the economy. This argument may be true in some circumstances but is clearly not in others. The North Sea oil and natural gas industry has supported many other industries from platform fabrication through to the most advanced engineering and computing. Back in 1999, the Venezuelan oil industry purchased $1.2 billion worth of domestically produced goods, while 4,500 companies, including 250 engineering and consulting firms and 2,750 manufacturers and distributors, supplied the industry, which indirectly provided work for perhaps one million people.[20] The government of President Lula da Silva in Brazil has encouraged domestic yards to compete for oil platform construction work as part of an effort to raise local content.[21] By contrast, in the Arab Gulf states linkage back into manufacturing is negligible; there is linkage forward into refining and petrochemical production, although much of the labour in these industries has traditionally been expatriate. In 2002 there were 10 million migrant workers in the countries of the Gulf Cooperation Council (GCC). Their remittances of $27 billion for the year almost matched the current account balance of the member countries. Over twenty-eight years some $413 billion was remitted rather than invested in the local economies, a boon for the generally poorer countries from which the expatriates originate but also a measure of the failure of the local economies.[22]

The windfall nature of the oil earnings of the 1970s (and perhaps the early years of this decade) created problems of its own. The additional revenues were massive, immediate and of indeterminate duration. The economies into which the revenues came faced difficulties absorbing them. That encouraged profligate and inflationary spending. Local businesses in Saudi Arabia, for instance, amassed fortunes in the 1970s from government contracts. Poor screening of projects meant the efficiency of investment worsened. In Nigeria, capacity utilisation in manufacturing, much of it government-owned, averaged 77 per cent in 1975, slid to 50 per cent in 1983 and has since fallen to 35–40 per cent, suggesting some two-thirds of investment has been wasted.[23] In Mexico, injudicious government investment left the state holding not just the steel and fertiliser plants of Lázaro Cárdenas but a cabaret, a bicycle factory and a biscuit maker. The number of state-owned enterprises mushroomed from 504 in 1975 to 1,155 in 1982.[24]

Inability to absorb windfall revenues saw major exporters build up vast funds. These have been used to establish funds for future use.[25] Of course, much of the windfall earnings went into worthy projects to develop education, transport, communication, housing and health. Infrastructure and human capital development accounted for some two-thirds of the spending in the countries Gelb studied. But much of the rest went into hydrocarbon and other resource-based industries. In some cases, this did provide a shield against future oil price falls.

Algeria, conscious of its limited reserves of oil, concentrated on building up its natural gas, chemicals and fertiliser industries such that while in 1980 crude oil accounted for 68 per cent of hydrocarbon exports, it accounted for just 25 per cent in 1984.[26] Nonetheless, industry in Algeria fell into chronic inefficiency – non-hydrocarbon industry operated at just 43 per cent of capacity in the early 1990s.[27] Indonesia bucked the trend in managing oil windfall revenues, and its agricultural and manufacturing bases achieved strong growth through a combination of 'good luck and an abundant supply of labour relative to oil income' and government policies that accepted the need for a flexible exchange rate and emphasised programmes to raise rural incomes, thus avoiding the Dutch disease.

Yet projects were often ill-planned, ill-managed and over-large. The white elephant of the Ajakouta steel mill has haunted

Nigeria for decades, epitomising time and budget overruns and redundancy. When oil, petrochemical and metals markets slumped in the early 1980s, the very sectors that had been invested in proved vulnerable.

As oil revenues fell away in the early 1980s, the windfall effect went into reverse. Non-oil output growth dropped off, investment was cut back, and prices rose as governments had to pare subsidies introduced in the boom years. Unable to judge how long the higher revenues would last or believing they would last for ever, governments were tempted to borrow against future revenues to fund expenditure. By the time prices began to fall in 1981, Mexico had a trade deficit of $3.7 billion due to imports of capital and intermediate goods.[28] Venezuela turned to the International Monetary Fund for help with a debt of $20 billion.

Coming further up to date, there is little to suggest that the governments of oil-dependent states have improved the performance of their economies since the bitter lessons of the early 1980s. GDP per capita growth rates have, by and large, been negative through the 1990s (albeit less so than for the last quarter of the century as a whole), while for developing countries as a whole and developing countries in every region except sub-Saharan Africa there was growth.[29]

For Nigeria, 'growth has been stagnant and per capita income is estimated to have fallen from about $800 in the early 1980s to about $300 today'.[30] Or, as another study put it,

> In 1965, when oil revenues per capita were about $33, per capita GDP was $245. In 2000, when oil revenues were $325 per capita, per capita GDP remained at the 1965 level. In other words, all the oil revenues – $350 billion in total – did not seem to add to the standard of living at all.[31]

From 1985 to 2000, the decline in Venezuela's per capita income accelerated. In Saudi Arabia, non-oil sector growth was only

1.2 per cent in the 1990s.[32] For the Gulf Cooperation Council members – Bahrain, Kuwait, Oman, Qatar, Saudi Arabia and the United Arab Emirates – between 1981 and 2001 income per capita fell from $18,000 to just $6,000.

Another indication of the failure to diversify is the lack of integration within oil-producing regions. The Gulf Cooperation Council grouping in 1981 signed an economic agreement calling for a free-trade area and harmonisation of development plans. In 1981, leaving aside the special relationship between Bahrain (which produces very little oil or natural gas) and Saudi Arabia, only some 4 per cent of the countries' trade was with each other and most of this was the re-export of goods from outside of the region.[33] In 2001 intra-group trade still accounted for just 6 per cent of their total.[34] After a spate of competing rather than complementary petrochemical projects – in effect, part of the oil and natural gas sector – diversification has been extremely limited, due in part to very low capital expenditure rates, in part to low private-sector participation, in part to low foreign direct investment in the group's members, and in part to the volatility of economic growth dictated by oil prices. The GCC registered GDP growth of minus 10.7 per cent in 1998, a positive 20.3 per cent in 2000 and a fall of 6 per cent in 2001.[35] Meanwhile, members run competing refineries, petrochemical plants, aluminium smelters, airlines and oil tanker operations.

The Maghreb Arab Union is more economically diverse, energy importer Morocco being one of the major members, but includes Algeria and Libya. Again, cross-border economic trade and co-operation have remained a dead letter.

In many oil- and natural-gas-exporting developing economies, lack of diversification is reflected and reinforced by the channelling of foreign direct investment flows towards the extractive industries. In 2003, Algeria's momentum of FDI inflows was due to

increasing exploration work. In Azerbaijan, a more than fivefold
increase in FDI was largely due to a 700 per cent rise in flow
to the oil sector. A doubling of foreign direct investment into
Brunei was dominated by money going into the natural gas and
oil industry.[36]

## Oil and poverty

Per capita GDP trends may indicate whether the wealth available to a society is increasing or declining, taking into account
population growth. But they say nothing about the distribution
of that wealth or about the standard of living of the population. The UN publishes an annual *Human Development Report*
that attempts to gauge social and economic development within
countries and then produce rankings that it combines into its
Human Development Index.

Data on income distribution is lacking for many countries,
notably Gulf Arab oil producers, but Kuwait, the UAE and Qatar
– all with small populations compared to their hydrocarbon
reserves – make it into the high human development category,
the top 48 of 162, as does Brunei. This indicates the achievement
of the massive spending on social infrastructure since the 1970s.
Mexico, Venezuela, Libya and Colombia all come high in the
medium human development category. For other oil producers,
the scores are less impressive. Saudi Arabia comes in at 68, Iran
at 90, Algeria at 100 (after years of civil strife), Nigeria at 136
and Angola (after decades of war) at 146.

What income distribution data is available for oil producers
suggests that income from oil has failed to filter down the social
scale and lift the poor out of impoverishment. In the Russian
Federation the richest 20 per cent account for 53.7 per cent of

consumption, while the poorest 20 per cent account for 4.4 per cent. For Venezuela the figures are 53.7 per cent and 4.1 per cent; for Algeria 42.6 per cent and 7 per cent; for Nigeria 55.7 per cent and 4.4 per cent. In the top 20 countries in the Human Development index the US figures are 46.4 per cent and 5.2 per cent for the richest and the poorest 20 per cent, respectively, and that is a considerably wider gap than for the other 19.

Indeed, there is an argument that oil wealth can increase the proportion of the population living in poverty, overpowering the beneficial effects of a statistical rise in per capita income. Ross found that countries with primary commodity dependence in 1970 were associated with unusually low life expectancy, high rates of child malnutrition and high poverty rates in the late 1990s.[37] The link held for metals- and oil-dependent countries but not for those dependent on food or non-food agriculture. The model Ross developed predicts that moving from a low-mineral-dependence state like Bangladesh to a high-mineral-dependence state like Zambia would produce a drop in life expectancy of 8.6 years, a rise in infant mortality of 32 deaths per thousand, an additional 12 malnourished children per thousand, and a rise of 40 per cent in the proportion of the population living below the poverty line. Moreover, the impact of a mineral discovery would be greater the poorer and smaller the country, according to the model. So, for Madagascar or Niger, a $1 billion a year mineral export project would increase poverty markedly as the negative effects of becoming more mineral export dependent outweigh the advantages of the increase in GDP per capita. In a relatively richer country like Saudi Arabia or Argentina, the positive and negative effects would almost balance each other out.

Ross suggests that the negative effects of metals and oil dependence come about in different ways. For metal exporters, it is an inhibition of economic growth that does the damage but for oil exporters it seems to be the reduction in the growth of manufacturing and the 'hindrance of democracy' that increase poverty.

## The petro-economies and the scramble for spoils

The depressing statistics of the economic failure of oil-exporting countries are inseparable from the political structure of those countries. The economic basis of the countries has determined the means by which political power and wealth are sought and won. The maintenance of power and wealth has then determined the distribution of part of the oil revenues and the consequences of that distribution subsequently feed back into political and economic life. In almost every country in the world – the US being the major exception[38] – subsoil wealth is owned by the nation via the central state. The state levies from producers – in this case oil and natural gas companies – 'rent' in exchange for the right to extract the finite natural resources. Whether the payment takes the form of a concession fee, a royalty on volumes produced, a tax on profits, or the state's slice of a production-sharing agreement, the revenue is still essentially rent, defined by economists as the profit from a differential advantage for production such as earnings from rare natural resources. The scarcity of the resource allows its owner to command a price greater than the cost of extracting the resource. Rent can also be extracted from transit infrastructure, making a case for counting Egypt as an oil rentier state due to its earnings from oil tankers passing through the Suez Canal.

Whether a country sits on mineral reserves or transit routes has generally been a matter of good fortune, given that borders have by and large been drawn prior to knowledge of or particular regard for hydrocarbon reserves (even if there have been numerous attempts to redraw them once oil and natural gas were discovered). To that extent, the wealth from oil and natural gas rents has appeared as what some commentators have called manna from heaven, easy money.

Because oil and natural gas extraction is capital- rather than labour-intensive and because their export to consumer countries requires little in the way of linkage into the rest of the local economy, production tends to create enclave industries (the well-meaning campaigns of industrialisation having been attempts to break down the walls of the enclave). Where the producer country is a developing country or where its hydrocarbon industry has burgeoned around the period of decolonisation, the industry has grown up with strong ties to the oil companies of the industrialised world. The run of nationalisations of the 1970s was an attempt to loosen or renegotiate these ties.

Where the state is well established and its legitimacy is recognised and respected by civil society, the accrual and deployment of oil and natural gas wealth can be transparent, as in Norway or the Canadian province of Alberta. But where the birth of the state (or its reconfiguration in the case of former centrally planned economies) coincides with or postdates the emergence of oil and natural gas exporting as the dominant sector of the economy, the interaction between the two is profound. Terry Lynn Karl reconciles the variety among oil-export-dependent states and the similarity of their economic failures through her concept of the petro-state:

> Petro-states are not like other states. While they share many of the development patterns of other developing countries, especially mineral exporters, the economies and polities of countries dependent on oil are rapidly and relentlessly shaped by the influx of petrodollars in a manner that sets them apart from other states. Oil wealth moulds institutions more dramatically than development specialists ever imagined or even

seem to understand. This is especially true if petroleum exploitation coincides with modern state building, as has so often been the case. Where this historical coincidence occurs, petro-states become marked by especially skewed institutional capacities. The initial bargaining between foreign companies anxious to secure new sources of crude and local rulers eager to cement their own bases of support – whatever their mutual benefits – leaves a legacy of overly-centralised political power, strong networks of complicity between private and public sector actors, highly uneven mineral-based development subsidised by oil rents and the replacement of domestic tax revenues and other sources of earned income by petro-dollars.[39]

Where a government derives its income from the taxable productive activities of its population it can expect its citizens to require some sort of accountability for the deployment of revenues. At some point, someone is likely to raise the slogan of 'No taxation without representation'. Elected governments are not re-elected if the voters disapprove of the level or use of taxes. Unelected governments, with the exception of those bent purely on short-term banditry, also have to blend mollification with repression if they are to survive.

Yet oil and natural gas revenues, because they are rents, because they largely derive from outside of the country, because they are channelled through an externally oriented, often externally financed enclave sector, impose far fewer constraints. The manna is there to be eaten by those who scramble to the table, or, as one study put it, 'rent reorients economic incentives towards competing for access' and away 'from productive activities, especially in non-transparent environments characterised by political discretion and unclear property rights'.[40]

The crumbs go to the lucky few local workers who can gain employment in the sector. The structure of the industry has allowed oil companies 'to buy-off oil workers with high salaries and create a type of aristocracy of labour'.[41] The bulk of the free lunch, however, is available for deployment by those in government or in control of government. Where the government is wholly unaccountable, the result is partisan allocation, misappropriation, plunder and corruption. Where there is some accountability, revenues are used to reward loyal constituencies and, if necessary, mollify others.

In Russia, the transition from Soviet rule to capitalism was marked by the transformation of powerful civil service barons into the oligarchs whose manoeuvrings dominate political and economic life in the country. One commentator remarked of Russia:

> Yet while privatisation may not have invigorated the energy sector, it did enrich those who presided over the process. Recognising the vast opportunities for personal gain, many of the apparatchiks in the newly formed energy ministry set aside at least a portion of the ministry's oil assets for privatisation while assuring themselves positions as chief executive officers and major stockholders in the new companies that controlled those assets.[42]

So natural gas industry minister Viktor Chernomyrdin became chief executive of Gazprom and was succeeded in that post by his former deputy minister Rem Vyakhirev. Vagit Alekperov created the giant company Lukoil, a predatory company that has sought to take over independent operations in Western Siberia.

The complex political stratagems, reminiscent of medieval court intrigues, of a handful of players were highlighted by the arrest of Mikhail Khodorkovsky, head of oil company Yukos, in late 2003 on charges of fraud and tax evasion on the most massive scale, charges widely believed to have been brought because he was perceived as a political threat to President Putin. Among the charges brought against Khodorkovsky was that of committing gross violations in the obtaining of oilfield licences in the early 1990s during the rule of President Yeltsin. Khodorkovsky, formerly a high flyer in the youth wing of the Russian Communist Party, bought Yukos when it was privatised in 1995, using his own bank Menatep in one of the auctions associated with the discredited loans-for-shares deals through which swathes of the Russian oil and natural gas industry passed into private hands at knock-down prices. In the same period, Boris Berezovsky, a Yeltsin favourite and Kremlin insider, acquired Sibneft. Berezovsky's downfall came when Putin succeeded Yeltsin. He was replaced at the helm of Sibneft by Roman Abramovich, who subsequently became governor of the remote Chukotka region of Russia, until recently a tax haven, further emphasising the interplay between political power and the reaping of oil and natural gas rents. Abramovich is a past master at the game of transfer pricing – buying up oil at controlled domestic prices and then exporting at higher market prices.

Moving down the food chain, the London-listed Anglo-Russian oil company Sibir has managed to avoid obstacles facing Western independents operating in Russia through an alliance with property developer Chalva Tchigirinski, a politically influential figure and a major shareholder. However, the alliance has dropped Sibir into the midst of internecine warfare between Russian companies.

The Russian oligarchs are entangled in the struggle to determine the political orientation of the country. Some, like the fallen Berezovsky, have resisted the entry of foreign capital into strategic projects. Deutsche Bank analysts wrote more recently that 'The Russian Oils are cash-rich and resurgent. They have low costs, low oil price thresholds, have little experience of partnerships and are unwelcoming to foreign partners in all but the most expensive and complex projects.'[43] Yet this did not prevent Russian nationalist parties from campaigning in the December 2003 parliamentary elections on vows to rein in the oligarchs with multibillion-dollar tax rises and so 'return the country's wealth to its people', a signal that the distribution of oil and gas rent has not been widespread enough to quell discontent. Indeed, a long-running dispute over the adoption of a new fiscal regime for the industry has been seen by some as a fight for access to oil rent between the energy ministry and the companies on the one hand and the finance ministry on the other. The decisions taken by Putin in respect of the oligarchs will indicate to what extent the development of Russian capitalism will be controlled by the state, as in China, and to what extent it will be driven by the oligarchs whose wealth derived from the dismantling of the public sector.

In Saudi Arabia oil rents have long been skimmed by the ruling royal family and its dependent caste. Said Aburish[44] points out that the family budget was published until the mid-1960s and quite openly showed it to average some 15–17 per cent of the national budget. He maintains the percentage is similar now. Certain members of the royal family are allocated volumes of oil to sell on as commission agents. So-called 'princely allocations' could amount to 1 million barrels a day, he says, citing a number of examples. Indeed, he asserts that the assigning of oil concessions to key figures in the regime has strained relations between the family and its oil ministers. Further, enabling the production and sale of additional volumes of crude in order to fund questionable business deals has even undermined Saudi pledges to OPEC. A World Bank-commissioned paper noted that the oil price collapse of the late 1990s, which severely squeezed the budgets of the Gulf's traditionalist autocracies, meant that

> Local discontent has been growing over unemployment and reductions in per capita income while privileged 'groups' are seen as basking in conspicuous consumption inconsistent with traditional values, and funded by the capture of an undue share of the remaining subsidies.[45]

In Latin America, where class and social factions are relatively well established and the populations larger in relation to the hydrocarbon reserves, the competition for control of oil rents is more complex. It is not just a matter of paying off the small local population with free health care and the guarantee of a salary from a desk job in a massively overstaffed bureaucracy while migrant workers keep the economy running. Rather, there are labour and business constituencies, rural and urban demands, regional requests, not to mention the need to keep all branches of the military onside. The paper quoted above says of Venezuela, 'Oil revenues have shaped Venezuelan politics for decades, creating a rentier state legitimised by patronage and entrenched constituencies whose continued loyalty is attached directly to state expenditures funded by oil rents.' Similar features of the rentier state are evident in Colombia and Ecuador.

Around a half of sub-national government revenues in Venezuela come, directly or indirectly, from oil. This is a cause of political and fiscal tension, with the central government wanting to claw back control. In Colombia, local administrations have become dependent on central government for some 50 per cent of their revenue, choosing not to exercise fully their tax collection powers.[46]

The coming to power of Hugo Chavez in Venezuela on the votes of the poorest sectors of Venezuelan society and the lower and middle ranks of the military introduced new contestants for access to oil revenues. Chavez set about trying to increase the government's yield from PdVsa, the national oil company, by raising the proportion of rent collected as royalties as opposed to taxes on income (deemed more difficult to audit). This, combined with Chavez's insistence on putting his own nominees onto a board hitherto dominated by managers with close ties to multinational oil companies, put the president on a collision course with the PdVsa hierarchy, which then joined opposition strikes against the government.

Of Turkmenistan, which is highly dependent on natural gas exported through Russia, a recent report said: 'most profits from these exports pass into the private bank accounts of the president and his close colleagues, with little reaching ordinary people.'[47]

Nigeria falls into the category of 'predatory autocracies' in Eifert, Gelb and Tallroth's typology of rentier oil states, with much of its post-colonial history comprising a series of coups aimed at securing a slice of oil revenues in a short space of time before making way for the next military strongman. As the country embarks on the export of its natural gas reserves, there is little reason to think the income they generate will not prove just as attractive. Okonta and Douglas write:

> Military coups in Nigeria are a zero-sum game. If you succeed, the prize is instant access to the billions of dollars of oil revenue extracted from the Niger Delta annually. If the coup is botched and you are caught alive to boot, the penalty is a swift court martial and summary execution. The glittering oil prize has, however, always proved an irresistible pull for Nigeria's ambitious and largely indolent officer corps, who, given the chance, are willing to walk the Valley of Death to seize it.[48]

In the eight-year rule of General Ibrahim Babangida some $12 billion was disbursed clandestinely, outside of the budget process. His second-in-command, General Sani Abacha, replaced him. Estimates of the wealth he creamed off range from $3 billion to $10 billion in a mere five years.

While very personalised self-enrichment has been particularly evident in Nigeria, in part because the military governments have been personified by single coup leaders, the reality has been more complex as each government, military or civilian, has had constituencies to satisfy. Indeed, the coup itself is merely a mechanism by which a new set of individuals replaces the existing set within a nexus of political and commercial relations.

More than twenty years ago, Terisa Turner examined the modus operandi of the strata that had ensured access to oil rents. She argued that the Nigerian state was controlled by a class of compradors, intermediaries who organise the access of foreign traders to the local market. They occupy positions within government and the

bureaucracy and so use public office to gain kickbacks and commissions on government contracts paid for with oil revenues.[49]

Trying to balance regional constituencies has been part of the
trick of ensuring control of oil rent. Nigeria's onshore oil reserves
are concentrated in the Niger Delta in the south. Expansion of the
civil service by the employment of northerners and the general
expansion of government as oil income rose was one way in which
the north sought to assert its control over resources located in the
south. The resentment of the people of the oil-producing areas
who suffer the pollution and land expropriation and repression
associated with Nigeria's oil industry is a live issue.

In 2000 alone, up to $1 billion in Angolan oil revenues was
spirited out of the country and into private bank accounts, according to a paper by the International Consortium of Investigative
Journalists, in a year when the country exported $6.9 billion
worth of crude.[50] Over that summer, a Jersey bank account of the
state oil company Sonangol made payments to a private security
company owned by a former minister, to a charitable foundation
run by the president, and to a private bank. Hodges refers to an
oil nomenklatura and a system whereby 'part of the rent for oil
has been transferred to the leading families of the regime through
such mechanisms as the rationed allocation of subsidised credit
by state banks and opportunities for kickbacks on oil-financed
contracts for military procurement'.[51] He adds that the beneficiaries
rarely invest their gains in long-term investments, preferring the
quick profits of import operations or foreign exchange dealing.

## Rent allocation and corruption: shades of grey

Where the economy is dominated by a sector that generates
rent, politics is dominated by the competition for rent, and
where institutions of government are not well established they

are liable to be wholly suborned by the interests of those who take control of them. But when do we cease referring to this process using nice academic terms such as 'competition for rent' and call it corruption?

President Chavez's electoral mandate allows us to portray the change in government in Venezuela as a victory of certain social strata over others in the competition for rent that is played out more or less imperfectly in periodic elections. In Russia, the seizure of access to oil and natural gas resources by the companies controlled by the oligarchs has been put under a legal cloud by President Putin as part of his political strategy, but, for all the dubious conditions in which some of the auctions took place, the process was set in motion with apparent legality at the time. By contrast, the Nigerian coup regimes are by definition unconstitutional; and Angolan law requires all foreign currency receipts and government revenues to go through the central bank, so Sonangol's role as an intermediary in government business, almost a state within the state, is illegal.

Yet does this get us anywhere? In the case of Angola, much of the money paid out by Sonangol from oil earnings went to service oil-backed loans taken out to finance the war against Unita rebels and reconstruction of the war-ravaged infrastructure, legitimate activities of an internationally recognised government (which is not to say that vast sums have not been creamed off by individuals in or close to government).

The case of Nigeria must be clearer: after $350 billion of oil revenue has accrued to government since 1965, the proportion of the population subsisting on less than a dollar a day has doubled from 36 per cent in 1970 to 70 per cent in 2000, while General Gowon's placemen raided the treasury and multiplied army salaries, and then venal and brutal strongmen like Abacha salted away billions.

Yet even the Nigeria case, it can be argued, is more complex. Chabal and Daloz employ the term 'corruption' and concede that the practice is 'nefarious' to the development of national economies. But they interpret (without fully defining) the practice as instrumental to society rather than dysfunctional, saying, for example,

> there is in Africa a marked reluctance to abide by the abstract and universalist norms of the legal-bureaucratic order that are the foundations of Western polities. The legitimacy of the formal rules of conduct which characterise the modern state has hitherto failed to supersede that of the informal compacts derived from ethnic, factional or nepotistic ties of solidarity.[52]

Citing a remark of the Ogoni activist Ken Saro-Wiwa, executed by Abacha, they continue: 'supporters will readily applaud when one of their own political leaders appropriates millions in the capital city but will at the same time expect him to be scrupulously honest in the management of his village finances.' Seeming dishonesty may be recast as a result of particular communitarian codes of conduct. In other words, rent channelled through established social chains, while not economically productive, is as normative as, say, the allocation of monies from Norway's oil fund to a part of the electorate through pensions.

The point here is certainly not to defend the plunder of revenues or the opaque bookkeeping that disguises it, but to re-emphasise that the process of gaining access to oil and natural gas rents and who gets that access are determined by the political institutions of the producer country. Where they are strong, access is controlled and predictable. Whether it is any fairer is a different matter.

Another aspect of 'corruption' is the interplay between foreign companies and states on the one hand, and between players in producer countries on the other. This subject is dealt with at length in an excellent report by the campaigning organisation Global Witness.[53] In recent years campaigns such as Publish What You Pay have nudged oil companies away from the position that backhanders, kickbacks and influence peddling are all part of doing business in the developing world. Now, companies like Shell and BP publish in glossy reports accounts of personnel sacked in a year for corruption. In 2000, the International Monetary Fund inaugurated an 'oil diagnostic' to identify and track Angolan government oil revenues as part of a reform programme required of the country. BP then came into conflict with the government in Luanda when it published details of signature bonuses (a form of up-front payment for exploration and production licences, criticised as particularly liable to diversion) it had paid.

Yet, despite these gestures, an air of murkiness hangs around the industry. In September of 2003, the chief executive of Statoil, Norway's national oil company, resigned as the Norwegian police and Iranian authorities launched an investigation into a ten-year, $15 million deal with a company owned by an expatriate Iranian consultant. According to Statoil, the Iranian introduced company officials to influential people in Tehran, where Statoil was seeking to build on a series of oil and gas development contracts.

In the same year in the US, ExxonMobil was under investigation over allegations that Mobil (prior to the merger with Exxon) paid a large portion of bribes worth $60 million to Kazakh president Nursultan Nazarbayev. The payments were allegedly made through a middleman, who, despite being indicted in New York, was rehired as a consultant to the Kazakh government.

The same year saw the Elf scandal come to a head. Three senior former executives, one-time chairman Loik Le Floch-Prigent, former director Alfred Sirven and the company's Africa head Andre Tarallo, were among those jailed. Many of the charges related to self-enrichment as gross as can be found anywhere in the world. The three were found to have personally misappropriated some €350 million between 1989 and 1993 to finance lavish lifestyles. Moreover, they did so, according to Le Floch, with the knowledge and protection of the Mitterrand presidency. At the same time, the company bankrolled political parties. But this stark reminder that self-enrichment on a grand scale cannot be laid at the feet of 'Third World dictators' alone is a sidebar to the main story, even if it was the aspect on which the French courts concentrated.

Elf was formed as a state oil company after the Second World War by French president Charles de Gaulle. Its stated role of maintaining independent French access to energy supplies accorded with other aims of the state and it became an informal arm of successive governments' foreign policy. Tarallo testified that large sums of money were paid out to heads of government in Africa (where Elf was particularly active) and their families. Countries named were Gabon (a major source of Elf's upstream profits), Angola, Cameroon and Congo–Brazzaville. The purpose of the payments was twofold: to ensure an advantage for Elf and to maintain countries' acquiescence in French military and espionage activities in Africa.

In Angola, Elf played both sides of the street in the civil war, paying both government figures and Unita leader Jonas Savimbi. In Gabon, it was suggested, Elf had a hand in bringing Bongo to power. In Congo–Brazzaville there were accusations that Elf arranged an oil-backed loan to finance arms imports by President Pascal Lissouba before his overthrow by Denis Sassou Nguesso.[54]

The US-led invasion and occupation of Iraq soon raised questions of linkage between contract awards, political donations and diplomatic decision-making. The Center for Public Integrity established that more than seventy companies and individuals had won contracts worth $8 billion for work in Afghanistan and Iraq. They had donated more money to the presidential campaign of George W. Bush than to any other politician in the previous twelve years. Engineers and service companies with deep roots in the energy sector, including Halliburton subsidiary Kellogg, Brown & Root,[55] and Bechtel, won work valued at over $3.3 billion.[56] Christian Aid remarked that contracts issued by Washington through USAID for Iraq's reconstruction, including the $1 billion contract secured by Bechtel,[57] lacked competitive process and denied Iraqi companies the opportunity to tender for business.

By the end of 2003, two divergent pulls were evident in US policy towards Iraq, the one to spread the cost of reconstruction by persuading other countries to invest and forgive debts accrued by Saddam's regime, the other to limit contract awards to countries that participated in the invasion and occupation. The interplay between the commercial interests and the political agendas of George W. Bush and key advisers, including vice-president Dick Cheney, former secretary of state James Baker, national security adviser Condoleeza Rice, and commerce secretary Don Evans is the subject of speculation. The Sustainable Energy and Economy Network and Institute for Policy Studies[58] documents a 'revolving door' between Bechtel and the Reagan administration. The main players then, in the 1980s, came to the fore under George W. Bush, pushing a pro-war line, it argues.

## Oil and civil conflict

That there is an interrelationship between the economic conditions of oil- and, by extension, natural-gas-exporting developing countries and the political structures of the countries has already been stated. Indeed it is evident in the distributive mechanisms of the rentier state just as it is in any other politico-economic system. However, in the case of the petro-state, the consequences are extreme – a tendency towards authoritarian, unaccountable government and a high likelihood of armed civil conflict. Whilst there is little to demonstrate that oil stimulates class conflict, there is plenty to suggest it incites secessionism within producer states and cross-border tension between states.

In his essay 'Does Oil Hinder Democracy?'[59] Ross notes that the thesis that oil impedes democracy has long been championed by Middle East analysts but not beyond the region, meaning the historical and cultural background of the region had not been ruled out as explanations. He set about examining whether there is a link between oil and anti-democratic rule, whether any such link is restricted to the Middle East, and whether oil has properties that other commodities lack.

The results of Ross's regression analysis are striking, suggesting that both oil and other mineral wealth are linked to anti-democratic trends in government.[60] The harmful influence of oil is not limited to the Middle East but 'has probably made democratisation harder in states like Indonesia, Malaysia, Mexico and Nigeria', and, looking ahead, 'it may well have the same effect on the oil-rich states of Central Asia' (and, presumably, other new oil producers in regions such as West Africa).

Just as his model of the impact of oil on poverty found that the negative effects of oil more quickly outweighed the positive effect of a rise in GDP per capita caused by a discovery in smaller-population and poorer countries, so his model of the impact of oil on democracy suggests that a discovery of a given value has more negative consequences in poorer and lower-population countries. Again, the predictive implications of the model for countries such as Chad, Mozambique, Equatorial Guinea and Mauritania are disturbing.

Ross also looked at three complementary causal mechanisms proposed as the links between oil and authoritarian rule: the rentier, repression and modernisation effects. Possible rentier effects are held to include the taxation effect mentioned earlier, as well as the spending effect – the conversion of oil revenues into patronage – and a group formation effect whereby, deliberately or not, regimes' deployment of patronage inhibits the development of civil society.

The repression effect argument holds that oil leads to larger military forces – either to defend the regime against its population or in response to ethnic or regional conflict engendered by oil wealth. The nub of the modernisation effect thesis is that democracy comes about through a range of social changes that include occupational specialisation and higher levels of education. Oil wealth may hinder or distort these changes.

The results of Ross's research suggested there was validity in all three of the mechanisms. There is a relationship between the level of taxation and the level of democracy (and rentier states derive relatively little from personal or corporate tax). The level of oil exports correlates with the level of military spending (though the same is not true for non-oil mineral exporters) but seems unrelated to racial, national or language divisions within a state. The evidence for the modernisation effect is more mixed – muddied by the traditionally high subsidisation of education in some of the Arab Gulf states.

The coincidence of oil and natural gas with civil conflict is intuitively obvious – Sudan, Angola, Yemen, Iraq, Colombia, Burma/Myanmar, Indonesia, Nigeria, Algeria, Congo–Brazzaville come quickly to mind. But in each case other factors – ethnic, linguistic, tribal, religious, colonial experience – are present. Also, there have been and are clearly many civil conflicts since the 1960s where hydrocarbons are not an obvious factor – Liberia,

Côte d'Ivoire, Sierra Leone, Rwanda, Kashmir, Nagorno Karabach, Lebanon, El Salvador, Nicaragua, the former Yugoslavia.

The link between conflict and natural resources – in particular, oil – has provided plenty of work for a cottage industry of analysts and economists. Foremost among these pundits is Paul Collier, whose highly economistic interpretation of civil conflict gained wider currency when the World Bank published it in 2000,[61] the interest perhaps generated in part by the campaign to control the 'blood diamonds' that fuelled wars in Africa.

Collier argued that the political grievances expressed by contesting parties in civil wars have little explanatory power in predicting where and when rebellions take place. Alongside low average incomes, slow growth and large diasporas, dependence on primary commodity exports, however, did have that explanatory power. Rebellion is the ultimate in organised crime rather than the ultimate in political protest, he contested. It is a predatory attempt to access wealth and the risk of conflict is determined by the feasibility of predation. Secession of resource-rich areas is a way to lock in access to rents, he argues, pointing to Biafra and Katanga as examples. With his colleague Anke Hoeffler, Collier identified 73 civil wars between 1965 and 1999 and found enough data to analyse 47.

A baseline country, average in every one of the characteristics examined, was found to have a 14 per cent chance of civil conflict over any five-year period. The most powerful risk factor found was having a substantial share of GDP deriving from the export of primary commodities. At the most dangerous level of dependence – found to be 26 per cent (later revised to 32 per cent[62]) – the risk of civil conflict rose to 23 per cent (revised to 22 per cent). Perhaps even more striking is that zero dependence on primary commodity exports reduced the risk to 0.5 per cent (revised to 1 per cent). Higher dependence on oil as opposed to other commodities increased the risk further.

Collier's rejection of political grievance as a factor in civil conflict has been revised. Indeed, his own work finds factors such as poverty, level of education, and ethnic division to be significant in predicting conflict. Economic reductionism served the purpose of showing the quest for rent and, in some cases, the access to rent for funding to be very important in many cases of rebellion but the superstructure of political discourse is crucial in moulding movements and determining their strategies. Collier himself noted in his policy recommendations that people are less likely to join a rebellion if a substantial proportion of natural resource revenue is seen to be going into local education rather than Swiss bank accounts – government action and deportment is important.

There are instances where a good case can be put for the argument that oil and gas have been major determinants in the decision to fight. The renunciation of decentralisation proposals by Nigerian coup leader Gowon was largely driven by concerns over loss of control over oilfields of the Eastern Region. That pushed the Igbo political leaders to declare the state of Biafra, leading to war and mass starvation. Okonta and Douglas note that one of Gowon's first moves as his troops took the oil-producing areas was to declare that all oil revenues would accrue to the federal government. Yemen's brief civil war in 1994 followed hard on the heels of a reunification of the country in 1990. It also followed the realisation by the southern political elite (apparently backed by Saudi Arabia), which was being subsumed by its northern 'partners', that the oil resources of the Hadramaut would finance a state more viable than the one they had just given up.

## Aceh

The series of secessionist uprisings in the Indonesian province of Aceh have been powered by the island's dependence on the liquefaction of natural gas for export.[63] From the beginning, in 1976, GAM (Aceh Freedom Movement) asserted that the wealth of Aceh (a relatively prosperous part of the Indonesian archipelago) was being plundered by the Javanese who dominate Indonesia as a whole. GAM opposed payment of royalties from natural gas production to the central government and there were resentments over employment levels generated by the LNG complex. There is evidence from 1977 onwards of GAM members attempting to levy money from the complex – most directly through a payroll raid.

By the time of the second phase of insurrection in 1989, natural gas and oil accounted for almost 70 per cent of Aceh's economy and there had been widespread dislocation of traditional ways of living. By the third phase a decade later, the GDP contribution was still around 65 per cent for an industry that employed just 0.3 per cent of the workforce.

The government in Jakarta, reeling from the Asian economic crisis of the late 1970s, in the process of losing East Timor to a pro-independence referendum vote, and seeing that the customary response of extreme brutality had strengthened rather than weakened Acehnese separatism, adopted new legislation. This included provision for regional governments to retain 30 per cent of net income from natural gas. It also provided for a large degree of cultural autonomy for Aceh. By 2001, Jakarta was offering the province 70 per cent of hydrocarbon earnings for a period of eight years. The fighting continued and Indonesian troops launched a major offensive in 2003.

A study by a Yale–World Bank joint project suggests that the looting of resources did not kick-start GAM, although extortion may have helped it to continue operations. But grievances over jobs and revenues from natural gas production and the LNG facility were influential, the presence of the LNG facility meant a heavier security presence and response (combined with military involvement in the plant), and the very scale of the revenues generated by LNG generates popular disbelief in Jakarta's promises of regional fiscal autonomy.

In another part of Jakarta's empire, BP is making strenuous efforts to prevent its Tangguh LNG project in Papua/Irian Jaya from becoming embroiled in an independence struggle in which the established extractive industries of logging and copper and gold mining are already mired, as government, military and commercial interests of the centre, local elites and popular resentments collude and collide. A second report by an advisory panel to the company reiterates that it 'is critical that BP establish a structure that is sustainable through political change that benefits all of the major political elements and thereby reduces incentives for any group to interfere with the project'.[64] Security around the plant is to be community based, and there is concern that Jakarta might declare Tangguh a 'vital national asset', which would 'trigger specific security obligations' by the army, presumably raising fears that the project would appear as compromised to the local inhabitants as does the plant in Aceh. The panel advises 'there is a greater need for visible benefits for the project's Papuan constituencies' as work on the plant progresses. Dialogue has created expectations that could turn to 'impatience' if unfulfilled.

## Angola

In Angola access to oil rent has underlain two conflicts since Portugal pulled out in the mid-1970s: the primary struggle for control of the central government, in which the combatant forces were whittled down to the ruling MPLA and Unita rebel forces, and a lower-key secessionist struggle in the oil-producing enclave of Cabinda.

The allure of the prize grows and grows as the country's revenues soar on the back of an extension of shallow offshore production into the Congo Basin and subsequent massive deep-water finds.

While Unita was funded by external powers and sales of diamonds from areas under its control, it was oil that financed the government's war effort and ensured its victory. With arrears and a low credit rating, the government could not raise bank loans but it could do so with oil revenues, with oil-backed loans and by awarding equity in oil projects to companies involved in arms dealing and financing. Jean-Christophe Mitterrand, son of the former French president, was arrested for involvement with an arms-for-oil deal with Angola in 1973.

Cabinda exported 500,000 barrels of Angola's 2000 output of 746,000 barrels a day. The coastal enclave lies within the territory of Congo–Brazzaville, Angola-proper being some thirty miles to the south. Even with the development of deep-water oilfields, Cabindan revenues will remain substantial and significant. As Hodges forcefully argues, oil revenues are the main driver of the Cabindan separatist movement:

> and also an iron-clad reason why the government, whether controlled by the MPLA, Unita or any other non-Cabindan party or ruler would never consider letting the province secede. For the Cabindans, the material benefits of secession would be quite staggering.... If it was an independent state, Cabinda would be one of the richest countries in the developing world in per capita terms ... a sort of African mini-Kuwait.[65]

## Sudan

In some cases oil and gas may not be significant factors in the commencement of hostilities but may, rather, legitimate existing conflicts or provide new justifications for their continuance. Sudan is a case in point. As Christian Aid put it:

Oil was not an original cause of Sudan's civil war, a conflict, in one form or another, that dates back almost 50 years. But oil was one reason that war resumed in 1983 and it has led to an escalation in fighting as the reserves, and the land above them, have become increasingly important to the government of Sudan. The oil fields are currently the only region of the country in which there is significant conflict.[66]

Or, as a regular reporter of the conflict put it:

> Until oil was discovered, Western Upper Nile was considered of little strategic importance. It was regularly affected by flooding and drought and its swampy terrain restricted conventional warfare. But with the discovery of oil in 1998, in areas accessible to the Northern government its forces began 'cleaning' territory inhabited by Southerners as a prelude to constructing roads that had a dual purpose: to open the way for oil exploration and to facilitate military advances.[67]

In the full-blooded civil war in Angola oil production has been all but undisturbed by the conflict because it is located offshore. In Algeria the oil and natural gas fields are deep in the desert and pipeline. In Sudan the oil is located in the regions contested by the government in Khartoum and the SPLA. That has led to a situation where the needs of the government army and the oil companies have frequently coincided or even become indistinguishable. So the oil companies have built roads that allow them to operate and at the same time facilitate military deployment. By the same token, the military has obliged the oil companies by ridding whole areas of potentially troublesome natives. US aid officials referred to a spring 2003 offensive by government forces as aiming to make the Western Upper Nile secure enough for Swedish oil company Lundin to resume operations.[68]

The oil companies have denied complicity in the catalogue of mass clearances, murder, rape and abduction in the oil-producing areas of southern Sudan but sometimes the denials have confronted the documentation, as in 2002 when a document emerged from the Petroleum Security Office in Khartoum. The papers asked for the armed forces to conduct cleaning-up operations around the Heglig oil field at the request of Canadian oil company Talisman.[69] A massive report published by Human Rights Watch 'provides evidence of the complicity of oil companies in the human rights abuses'.[70]

Pressure from lobby groups, the threat of US sanctions and the difficulties of operating in a war zone gradually convinced Western oil companies to withdraw from the country. Arakis sold out to fellow Canadian company Talisman its portion of the acreage Chevron gave up in 1985. In October 2002, Talisman sold its Sudan assets to ONGC of India for $758 million. Lundin of Sweden and OMV of Austria followed suit. But this did not inconvenience the Sudanese government. Since 1999 the trade balance has turned positive, oil now accounts for some 70 per cent of export earnings, and production in 2003 hit 300,000 barrels a day and remains on an upward trajectory. In addition to, and more significant than, further European and Canadian companies willing to invest in Sudan while fighting continued, Indian, Chinese and Malaysian oil producers have moved in.

Oil earnings have, of course, funded Khartoum's war effort. Some 60 per cent of the $580 million of oil revenues received in 2001 was absorbed by the military.[71] And the increased importance of Asian oil companies has coincided, in the case of India at least, with a willingness to provide military support to the Sudanese government. On 14 December 2003, it was reported that India had offered military training and equipment for the Sudanese army, navy and air force, even as the Khartoum regime negotiated with its adversaries.[72] The following day, it was reported that the Indian oil minister was to visit Sudan to discuss a number of projects.[73]

In January 2004, the Sudanese government and the SPLA signed an agreement seen as heralding a full peace settlement. The major item in the preliminary deal was the stipulation that net oil revenues from production in southern Sudan would be split fifty–fifty during a six-year transitional period. Having determined that neither could win and with Khartoum anxious to mend fences with Washington, the main protagonists resolved to divide the oil rent between themselves.

## Colombia's tribal peoples

The Sudanese conflict has been vast and bloody, bringing death to perhaps 2 million people in the last two decades and involving the displacement of hundreds of thousands from oil-producing areas in the last few years. Elsewhere the numbers have been far smaller but the potential consequences for communities equally fatal. Take, for example, the U'wa people of the Colombian Andes, a community whose struggle for survival is treated as a sidebar to the main story of conflict between a fascistic government backed by death squads and leftist guerrilla groups. As the Rainforest Action Network said:

> Throughout Colombia, oil and violence are closely linked. Colombia's left wing guerilla groups view oil industry installations as strategic targets in a three decade war between guerilla factions and the government. In response the government has militarised oil production and pipeline zones, making oil industry installations ground zero in Colombia's ongoing civil war. Oil projects have already taken their toll on many indigenous peoples of Colombia, including the Yarique, Kofan and Secoya.[74]

Confronted on the one hand by Occidental Petroleum of the US, and on the other by their belief that their land is sacred, the U'wa threatened collective suicide if drilling went ahead. In this instance, backed by a substantial international campaign, the indigenous people won at least a respite. In May 2002, Occidental's shareholder meeting decided to relinquish the acreage covering U'wa land after one well failed to find oil or natural gas. Meanwhile, Occidental's Cano Limon pipeline continued to leak oil into the rivers and lakes to the north of U'wa land and to attract attacks from guerrilla groups, 500 in its first twelve years of operation.

## Nigeria

Nigeria is Africa's most populous state. Its main onshore oil- and natural-gas-producing region comprises a patchwork of communities of varying sizes, some related to larger linguistic and ethnic groups, others not. Nigeria as a whole comprises some 100 million people divided between 200 ethnic groups. In 1995, the execution of Ken Saro-Wiwa, leader of the Movement for the Survival of the Ogoni People (Mosop), and eight of his colleagues drew attention to one aspect of the struggle within Nigeria for access to oil revenues. The Ogoni people's territory had long been exploited for oil. Shell's output was running at 30,000 barrels a day in the early 1990s. Mosop was formed in 1990, and in 1992 it issued demands that Shell, Chevron and the Nigerian National Petroleum Corporation pay $6 billion in back-royalties plus $4 billion compensation for the undoubted devastation caused to their land; that there should be a cessation of gas flaring; and that oil pipelines should be buried.

Enormous demonstrations, vigils and an election boycott backed Mosop's demands. But the military rulers Babangida and Abacha (with an interregnum of Ernest Shonekan) were hardly likely to give ground. From mid-1993 Ogoni communities began to come under attack by troops. Mosop sympathisers say that Shell-armed and -financed police units and company vessels were used in some attacks. In the first two weeks of September 2003 alone, according to Okonta and Douglas, 1,000 Ogoni were killed in three villages and 20,000 made homeless.[75]

Shell ceased operations in Ogoni territory during the height of the Ogoni protests, yet is now anxious to return to an area where production costs are estimated to be as low as $3 a barrel.[76]

The protests of the Ogoni are only the best publicised of those of the communities in Nigeria's oil-producing region. Activists from Niger Delta communities attempt to work together to form a front to press common demands. In late 2003, several women's groups planned a cross-community grand meeting for 2004 to coordinate activity. In 2002 and 2003 women from the oil town of Warri hit the headlines when they occupied an oil installation at Escravos and blockaded the site of a proposed naval base, protesting at the level of benefit their community received from oil operations in the area.

The rhetoric of some of the Delta community organisations has begun to raise the spectre of secession, something the federal authorities and, indeed, the northern elites could not begin to consider acceptable under any circumstances. The oil industry newspaper *Upstream* in February 2003[77] cited the leader of a group called the Association of Niger Delta Communities threatening to withdraw from the federation and perhaps even seek to join neighbouring Cameroon (with which the Abuja government has had territorial differences). A few months later, the same paper quoted another community activist, saying: 'There is a feeling that the Nigerian federation is nearing endgame with the time of break-up looming. I don't want that but we'll soon arrive at a point where we must question whether Nigeria should even hold together.'[78]

The clash between Delta communities on the one side, and Shell (and other oil companies to a lesser extent) and the Nigerian government (for which, as operator of a joint venture with the state oil company, Shell is seen as a local proxy) on the other, is relatively uncomplicated. The environment of the land and waters of many parts of the Niger Delta has been devastated by oil production. The local populations want compensation and the cessation of damaging activity, and believe they are not receiving an adequate share of wealth produced through the exploitation of natural resources beneath the land and water they have traditionally lived off.

However, competition for access to oil revenues has set community against community, generating or exacerbating conflicts that are both bloody and complex. The fulcrum of this violence since 1997 has been Delta State, which produces 40 per cent of Nigeria's oil. There, militias of the Ijaw, Itsekiri and Urhobo ethnic groups have fought for control of two revenue streams. The first is the stream from central government, which returns 13 per cent of proceeds of production from the state to the local government, meaning that positions gained through election are powerful instruments of patronage. The second is the proceeds of oil tapped illegally but on an industrial scale from pipelines running across the territory. Somewhere between 150,000 and 300,000 barrels a day are siphoned off, loaded onto barges and smuggled out of Nigeria for sale in neighbouring countries, including Benin and Côte d'Ivoire. Taking the midpoint of the estimates, this massively profitable exercise accounts for 10 per cent of national production and is worth hundreds of millions of dollars each year. The practice is tolerated by successive federal and state regimes and is widely held to continue because of the direct complicity of senior figures.

Inter-communal rivalries and jealousies feed into and off competition for control of this 'bunkering' business, so that:

> The fight for control of illegal bunkering opportunities has also significantly escalated the violence in Delta State and worsened the human rights abuses suffered by its people. Oil has become literally the fuel for the violence – despite the fact that in theory it should be easy to stop its theft (it is hard to hide a tanker and easy to trace its owner).

Some clashes in the creeks appear to have no political component whatsoever, but are simply a straight fight for opportunities to steal oil; in other cases, motives are mixed.[79]

In 2003 alone the clashes caused hundreds of deaths, while thousands of people were displaced. When the violence reaches a high pitch or spills over into the kidnapping of oil company staff or contractors, the result is counterproductive to the sponsors of the militias. For example, by late March 2003, ChevronTexaco, Shell, and TotalFinaElf had shut in production totalling 800,000 barrels a day while staff had been evacuated. As financial news agency staff well know, first reports of disruption of production or loading activity in Nigeria frequently cause moves on the international oil futures markets.

## Local versus national government

As remarked above, control of local government shares of oil revenue is keenly and often illegally contested in the oil-producing region of Nigeria. The value and vehicles of official revenue distribution are subject to scrutiny and change in many producer countries where demands from communities in producer areas may demand compensation for disruption to their lives or insist that they have a greater right to revenues than does central government. This latter insistence is insidious because it raises deeper political questions about rights to rent, and about the legitimacy of the central state and, indeed, of existing local and national boundaries. In Indonesia, districts within five provinces would receive some 80 per cent of revenues if they were distributed on the basis of origination, while the other twenty-five provinces would share the balance. In 1997 in Russia the five richest regions, with just 5.5 per cent of the population, collected 53 per cent of all sub-national revenues from natural resources.[80] Within the United Kingdom the location of the bulk of oil off the coast of Scotland provided Scottish nationalists with an important weapon with which they could point to an unfairness – Scottish oil funding a London government – and a source of income for the posited independent Scotland. As one study noted, 'Revenue sharing also does not diffuse separatist tendencies, since oil-producing SNGs [sub-national governments] would still be better off by keeping their oil revenues in full.'[81]

In Nigeria, at present, some 13 per cent of monthly federal oil revenue goes to producer states through local government or through the Niger Delta Development Commission, successor to the corrupt and discredited Oil Mineral Producing Areas Development Commission and Petroleum Task Force. This is on top of the revenue assigned to those states using the formula applied to all states of the federation. Some of the oil-producing states argue that all revenues deriving from their territory should accrue to them, while others are calling for a share of the revenues of the new deep offshore oil and natural gas fields.

The need to find a way out of the inefficiency, inequality, corruption and violence engendered by the competition for oil revenues at state level in Nigeria is underscored by the prospects of exploitation of the country's vast natural gas reserves, otherwise that new source of income will prolong the problems deriving from oil production. A controversial proposal put forward in recent years was to allocate revenues to individual adults rather than to government units while dealing with issues such as compensation for damage to the environment of producing areas through normal tax and expenditure methods.[82] The practicality of the proposal is open to question.

Revenue-sharing between local and national governments is problematic at the fiscal and the political levels, whether one looks at the extreme example of Nigeria or more broadly. At the fiscal level it tends to introduce a high degree of volatility into local government revenues, with all the attendant problems for planning and risks of indebtedness. It also extends the problems associated with primary commodity export dependence further into the economic fabric, creating another layer of government that is dilatory about tax collection and accountability. At the political level, revenue assignment by central government and lower levels of local level tax collection increases the dependency of the local government on the national government, implying relationships of patronage.

## Oil and labour

Inasmuch as oil and natural gas export dependence hinders the development of other sectors of the economy, it may also forestall the conditions necessary for the development of a broader labour movement even if the sector itself becomes organised along classical lines. And if the sector itself comprises an enclave, and one with low labour and high capital intensity at that, within an increasingly undeveloped or stultified host economy, its ability to infect other, weaker sectors with notions of industrial labour organisation is presumably very limited.

A description of the sector's operations in the Middle East and North Africa describes well the enclave nature of oil and natural gas production:

> it not only supplies its own fuel and generates its electricity but also carries its oil by pipeline and loads it on to tankers by submarine pipelines, forms of transport that cannot be used for any other purpose and that do not create external economies. The location of the oil fields in inhospitable and largely uninhabited areas, has further insulated the industry from surrounding economies and societies.

This was reinforced by the backward state of those economies and societies, which greatly reduced the linkages between them and the industry. This situation forms a sharp contrast to the one in developed countries, where petroleum has tight linkages, forward and backward, with the rest of the economy.[83]

Defining the scale of employment generated by the sector is not that straightforward. The Nigerian National Petroleum Corporation employs just 13,000 staff although the operating companies employ many more. Saudi Aramco, the monopoly producer in Saudi Arabia, employs only 56,000 staff. PdVsa in Venezuela, with 80,000 staff and direct contractors in 1999, accounted for between 1 and 3 per cent of employment in the country. In Algeria the sector accounts for only around 50,000 direct jobs.

The complication in counting heads comes with deciding whether to add in contractors, in which case should that only be contractors directly tied to the sector – those working for drilling companies, for example – or include those in shipyards or caterers, for whom the industry provides some work? Should the local watchmen taken on by companies operating in Yemen as insurance against vehicle hijackings and other ways of garnering a tiny share of the rent be counted? At the time of the 1979 Iranian revolution, this problem of definition produced a range of 19,000 to 78,000 in estimates of the number of oil workers.[84]

Giusti, a former head of PdVsa, provides the 80,000 figure cited above but probably exaggerates when he argues that more than a million jobs, a quarter of the total in Venezuela, are accounted for by the demand exercised by the oil and natural gas industry.[85]

What is certain is that the core workforce that operates fields, pipelines, refineries, and export terminals in export-dependent countries comprises a small, well-paid elite within the local working class, capable of shutting down one of the major sources of government revenue. This being the case, it is surprising that little comparative work has been done on the role of organised labour across producer countries. Do workers in the sector tend to use their muscle simply to advance workplace demands – wages, working conditions? Does the strategic importance of the industry they operate in imbue economistic demands with a political edge? Do oil workers veer towards overtly political action and, if so, can this be categorised? Can useful comparisons be made between, say, the resistance of Algerian workers to proposals for reform in the industry and that of their peers in Nigeria? The following paragraphs do not answer these questions but may further point up the scope for research.

In many oil- and natural-gas-producing countries, trade-union organisation is either banned, as in the UAE, circumscribed to the point of being banned, as in Saudi Arabia, or severely restricted, as in Kuwait. Nonetheless, a cursory search through the archive of the industry newspaper *Upstream* for the year 2003 quickly produces stories of industrial action in Algeria, Venezuela, Nigeria, India, Ecuador, Pakistan, Colombia, Indonesia and Norway.

Some of these actions were over traditional union concerns, like that in August 2003 when Indian workers at the Oil and Natural Gas Corporation protested after a fatal helicopter crash offshore Bombay, or the April strike threat at Caltex Pacific Indonesia over company attempts to change the work roster, or the Colombian oil workers' strike warning when company Ecopetrol said it would invoke a tribunal after a negotiating time limit expired.

Others involved defence of communal rights or union representatives. So, in Pakistan natural-gas industry workers staged a strike in April, saying the employers had reneged on promises to provide jobs and benefits, including housing and provision of natural gas and electricity to villages close to the fields. In Colombia, the most dangerous country in the world for trade-union activists, workers staged a 24-hour strike to protest against an arrest warrant issued against a union official said to have links with a guerrilla group and already the target of one assassination attempt by right-wing militias.

Nigeria's unions – blue-collar Nupeng and white-collar Pengassan – continued their wage militancy with the staff union picketing TotalFinaElf, for example, and Nupeng members taking a hundred expatriate workers hostage on four drilling rigs in a wildcat action during a dispute with drilling contractor Transocean.

The Nigerian unions have a history of militancy that extends firmly into the political sphere. In 1993, the leaders of Nupeng and Pengassan were imprisoned and replaced by administrators appointed by the Babangida junta during a strike over the annulment of elections. More recently, sections of Nigeria's organised oil workers have taken action against the removal of retail fuel subsidies. Then, having won a respite on that issue, the Nigerian Labour Congress, which has close structural ties to the oil unions, attacked government plans to privatise the country's four refineries, suggesting their low capacity utilisation allowed powerful figures in the oil corporation and politicians to profit from oil product importation. 'We need supply targets, not price targets. We'll never get the right price due to volatile markets and the downward pressure on the naira, so we need to get our refineries working and even export product', the NLC president said,[86] going on to add that downstream reform required an improved regulatory environment, thereby clearly and deliberately straying into the area of political policy. Unions have also called for the establishment of a reserve facility for windfall gains from oil price increases. Moves by Shell to transfer a number of white-collar jobs abroad brought accusations from the unions of racist policies aimed at sidelining local professionals, and the unions resurrected the issues surrounding the failed 'Nigerianisation' policies of earlier governments.

Privatisation plans attracted the opprobrium of oil workers' trade unions in sub-Saharan Africa, North Africa and Latin America in 2003. The case of the Nigerian refineries has already been mentioned. In Algeria, February brought a two-day general strike that included oil- and natural-gas-sector workers even though the energy minister's plans to commercialise state corporation Sonatrach had been shelved two months earlier. Their banners included the slogan 'A weak Sonatrach is a weak Algeria.' A driving fear was the customary one that commercialisation would result in the sort of job losses seen in the agrifood industry when that was privatised and 60 per cent of workers lost their jobs.[87] Mid-year in Ecuador there was a nine-day strike over government plans to allow further participation by foreign companies through joint-venture deals after simple service contracts failed to boost the country's flagging output. In each of these cases, defensive union action clearly challenged the government's ability or prerogative to determine policy for a strategic industry.

Yet it was in Venezuela in 2003 that oil workers' action was the most explicitly political. The wage round had already been settled when some 30,000 PdVsa employees, led by middle and senior managers, joined an opposition strike aimed at removing Hugo Chavez from the presidency. 'Stripped down to the essentials, we can say that a company is trying to bring down a government, and that is quite a tall order', *Upstream* quoted Petroleum Finance Company analyst Roger Diwan as saying.[88] Venezuela's exports of some 2.7 million barrels a day were all but wiped out, as was its refinery output, which usually ran at 1 million barrels a day. The senior managers of the company objected to Chavez's move to put nominees of his own on the board of the national oil company. His policy of close cooperation with other OPEC members to support prices also ran counter to the previous Venezuelan government and PdVsa policy, which sought to loosen links between the country and OPEC policy.

The strike hit government earnings and disrupted established oil flows but had little effect on Chavez's constituencies in the *barrios* and barracks of the country. In its wake, many PdVsa employees were sacked and there were reports of blacklisting. Meanwhile, key opposition organisers sought refuge in Colombia, El Salvador and Costa Rica. US involvement in the attempt to bring down a government it opposed was denied by Washington. On the face of it, the labour aristocracy, in the shape of a large proportion of PdVsa employees, had thrown in its lot with an opposition sponsored by Venezuelan private business interests and a privileged middle class and at the very least tacitly supported by Washington.

A quarter of a century earlier, oil workers had played a major role in bringing down the government of the shah of Iran. Their participation (and that of other sections of the organised industrial working class, like the steel and rail workers) lagged behind other parts of the population[89] but was decisive when it came, shutting down national production of 5.7 million barrels a day and bringing on the so-called second oil price shock. The oil workers' demands were political, among them an end to martial law, release of political prisoners, and dissolution of the security organisation SAVAK. Exports to apartheid South Africa and Israel were targeted by the strikers. The oil workers, according to contemporary accounts, threw up radical representatives, who quickly found themselves at odds with the clerical leadership that emerged from other parts of the Iranian Revolution. For some, 'The oil workers shut down the industry on behalf of the whole population, and thereby dispelled the myths about the conservatism of the labour aristocracy and the economism of the modern proletariat.'[90]

## Cross-border tensions

That social and political relations within recognised national boundaries are relatively sacrosanct — the principle of non-interference in domestic affairs — is a corollary of the sanctity of the often colonially imposed borders themselves. The exception is where might outweighs international law. So, US support allowed — at least while expedient — the South African occupation of Namibia; Israel's occupation of the West Bank, Gaza Strip, Golan Heights and South Lebanon; Morocco's occupation of the Western Sahara; and Indonesia's occupation of East Timor.

The oversight of relations between states by the UN, regional bodies such as the African Union, and the International Court of Justice, moderates and mediates cross-border conflict over oil and natural-gas resources but does not remove the risk of conflict.

Where Europe's rush for the natural resources of Asia, Africa and the Americas engendered conflict with indigenous peoples and between competing colonial powers, since decolonisation those conflicts have been devolved to local, successor states of the colonial entities. The lure of rent from exports to the North generates and sustains competition for natural resources between the successor states.

The late 1990s saw a rush for oil and natural gas in the Gulf of Guinea off the coast of West Africa. The subsequent scramble to claim rights over marine acreage resulted in more than thirty territorial disputes. Most of these have been or will be resolved amicably. A joint commission operates exploration affairs across the marine frontier of Senegal and Guinea Bissau, for example. But when the International Court of Justice in the Hague ruled in 2002 that the Bakassi Peninsula belonged to Cameroon and not to Nigeria, the Abuja government rejected the verdict and popular passions were whipped up with thousands of youths from the disputed territory volunteering to enlist in the Nigerian armed forces.[91]

When Morocco and Mauritania occupied the Western Sahara in 1975 as Spain withdrew, the established wealth of the territory was phosphates, raising concerns that Morocco wanted to establish itself as the dominant global producer and price fixer of a market that was then booming. More than a quarter of a decade later, with oil discoveries offshore Mauritania to the south, and Morocco once more suffering financially from its total dependence on imports of oil and natural gas, the kingdom offered licences to TotalFinaElf of France and Kerr McGee of the US, covering the entire territorial waters of the Western Sahara. A major diplomatic row and a UN legal decision on the inadmissibility of outside powers exploiting the resources of non-self-governing territories ensued; nevertheless seismic data has been collected and the prospect of oil has given Morocco a new incentive to maintain its occupation.

In the South China Sea, the 500-mile chain of rocks known as the Spratly Islands is subject to territorial claims by no fewer than six countries interested in the unproven natural-gas and oil deposits lying beneath and around them. China, Vietnam and Taiwan claim sovereignty over all of the chain, while the Philippines, Malaysia and Brunei claim a part. The navies of China and Vietnam clashed over the Spratlys in 1974 and 1988. Relations were normalised in the early 1990s but the issue of the Spratlys was not resolved and a row broke out in 1992 when the two countries issued overlapping exploration permits to US oil companies. As China's voracity for oil and natural gas grows, so will its determination not to relinquish its claim to what its geologists believe to be multibillion-barrel reserves.

In the Caspian region, a territorial dispute between Iran and the other littoral states of Azerbaijan, Kazakhstan, Turkmenistan and Russia has delayed work by oil companies and set the right-wing US think-tank the Heritage Foundation calling on George W. Bush to intervene diplomatically and militarily by expanding Azerbaijan's capability and ties with NATO.[92] Iran questions the maritime and seabed demarcation of its sector of the Caspian Sea and has also raised the question whether the Caspian should be treated as a lake or a sea, the two having different legal regimes. Tehran claims sovereignty over 20 per cent of the Caspian, whereas prior to the collapse of the Soviet Union its sector comprised 12 to 14 per cent of the total. In 2002, Azerbaijan agreed to stop exploration on the disputed Araz-Alov-Sharg field; a year earlier Iranian gunboats had forced a vessel working for BP off the field.

In the Arabian Gulf, a number of oil- and natural-gas-related territorial disputes come to the surface from time to time: United Arab Emirates disputes with Iran; Saudi and Yemeni disagreements over border demarcation; and, until recently, a row between natural-gas-rich Qatar and hydrocarbon-poor Bahrain over the Hawar islands, only resolved after a ten-year court battle.

More dramatic was the August 1990 invasion of Kuwait by Iraqi forces. While Iraq had claimed sovereignty over its small southern neighbour since the early 1960s and garnered some popular support for this from pan-Arab nationalists, the impetus for the 1990 invasion was largely financial. The decade of war with Iran had left Iraq heavily indebted to other Arab regimes, particularly Saudi Arabia and Kuwait. Meanwhile, the price of oil had inexorably deteriorated and was being further weakened by overproduction by Kuwait. Indeed, Iraq was pushing OPEC to try to raise prices in the months before the invasion.

At the same time, Kuwait and Iraq were in dispute over the cross-border Rumaila field. Iraq had refused to discuss a division of production costs and revenues. After the end of the Iran–Iraq war, Kuwait declined to negotiate over either the debt or the oil reserves. During that war, Iraq had mined the majority of the field that lay within its borders to prevent it falling into Iranian hands, but Kuwait increased its pumping from Rumaila, tying the issue of the field to that of Kuwaiti overproduction and the downward pressure on prices. Saddam Hussein claimed Kuwait owed Iraq $2.4 billion and was conducting economic warfare against Iraq.[93]

While the political objectives of stealing the Arab nationalist cloak, winning an easy victory after the bloody failure of his invasion of Iran, combined with the strategic aim of securing Gulf coastline, there is a strong argument that oil and indebtedness, along with signs of US indifference, persuaded Saddam Hussein to wipe out part of his debt and appropriate Kuwait's 1.8 million barrels a day of production.

Surveying all of this evidence of the stresses, inequalities and injustice that have accompanied dependence on oil export and will likely attend gas export dependence, the justification for the colourful phraseology cited at the beginning of this chapter is evident. Hydrocarbons too often endow the touch of Midas. But whereas Midas reaped both the gold and the misery, for exporting countries wealth goes to some and misery to many. And there lies the nub of the problem. Rent as a predominant form of national income is particularly liable to lack of transparency and partisan distribution. At the same time, control of rent enables and reinforces political (and military) control.

That said, it would be as absurd for people of a hydrocarbon-rich country to wish away their resources as it would be for those in a resources-poor country to wish idly for them. Undoing the spell of the 'commodity curse' is a political project. That project can only be achieved through the construction of social institutions that impose transparency on the collection and distribution of hydrocarbon wealth. The nature of rent means that the only way this can be achieved is through the widest popular participation in decision-making. Achieving that poses different problems for different societies. For some it means confronting ethnic divisions, for others regional issues, for others traditions of rule by families or military cliques. Elsewhere the issue will be expressed in terms of class. As if this did not pose challenges enough, the strategic nature of hydrocarbons means no population will be left to determine its own social structures. As the next chapter discusses, for the big powers oil and gas are too important to be left to their owners to manage.

# 3

# Oil security and global strategy

Oil is the one strategic commodity of the world that governments, from superpowers to minor states, will never allow to be free of political control.

Youssef M. Ibrahim[1]

The enticing prospect of freedom from the whims of foreign rulers has been held by every president since 1973 and its infamous Arab boycott. Our energy security is also directly linked with the voracity of OPEC's demands. OPEC ... conspires to fix prices and restrict the supply of crude oil to the world market in order to maximize profits. We must devise alternate sources of energy and supplies to confront this threat.

US congressman Henry Hyde[2]

In dealing with foreign policy, because we mess up our energy policy, we have this so-called great need to defend our oil, and it drives our foreign policy. Whether it is in Colombia to protect a pipeline, whether it is in Venezuela to have our CIA involved, whether it is in the persistent occupation of the Persian Gulf (which does not serve our interests), whether it is in the expansion of our occupation of Central Asia, whether it is in our control of where and how the oil comes out of the Caspian Sea, and possibly our presence in Afghanistan, may all possibly be related to energy.

US congressman Ron Paul[3]

Our economic well-being depends on secure energy supplies at affordable prices for the UK and world economies. We will need to improve the long term efficiency and stability of the international energy market through political and economic reform in key supplier and transit countries.

UK Foreign and Commonwealth Office[4]

As these recent quotes indicate, a secure supply of energy – and for now that means oil and, increasingly, natural gas – is a key strategic objective of consumer-country foreign policy. Although the intensity of energy use – the amount of energy consumed relative to productivity – in developed countries has fallen with increased efficiency and the migration of manufacturing industry to cheaper labour pools in the developing world, total demand keeps growing and dependence on imported energy persists.

Over the past half-century, again and again oil has been a major factor in international crises, from the overthrow of Mussadeq in Iran and the Suez Crisis in the 1950s, to the 1973 price rises and the short-lived Arab embargo of the same year, the impact of the Iranian Revolution on prices in 1979, the tanker war of the 1980s, the Gulf crises of 1990 and 2003. For Britain, dependence on oil from Persia – modern-day Iran – diluted dependence on coal from domestic pits, even if it was not until near the end of the twentieth century that the power of organised labour in the pits could be smashed.

In the first years of the last century, the navies of the imperial powers shifted from coal to oil. Daniel Yergin, whose book *The Prize* succeeded Anthony Sampson's *The Seven Sisters* and Peter Odell's *Oil and World Power* as the popular read on the oil industry, made the much-quoted observation, 'I think we can say that the era of energy security began when Winston Churchill converted the British navy from coal to oil on the eve of the First World War.'[5] Britain and Germany (and France and Belgium) went to war in 1914 as coal producers that would increasingly opt for oil as the fuel of choice. They lacked domestic sources of oil but with development of armoured and aerial warfare would become ever more militarily dependent on oil, guaranteeing that their competition would engulf producer regions in intrigue, colonial exploitation and war. With the development of the cheap internal combustion engine, the centrality of oil to economic as well as military security became definitive.

The parameters and the players in the quest for security of energy supply, as defined by the governments of the major consumer nations, change with and play upon the geostrategic shifts of the past hundred years. This means the optic through which energy security is seen in Washington or London or Paris or Tokyo changes. The US now courts Russia as an oil supplier where once it lobbied NATO allies not to buy Soviet crude. China, once inconsequential to oil politics, is on the cusp of demonisation in the US as its role in world oil markets grows.

The early years of the last century saw the commencement of the long-running competition for access to Middle Eastern crude through the concession system whereby oil companies supported by their governments pressed weak and dependent local governments and leaders to grant monopoly exploration and production rights. Much of the time, who would operate in this or that region was determined by discussion between European governments over the heads of the locals. After the Second World War the US was in a strong enough position in relation to Europe to ensure its full participation in the exploitation of oil reserves in the Middle East. Where the European powers had been dependent on external sources of oil from the start (though Britain would become a major net exporter for some years after the North Sea discoveries of the 1970s), the US as the world's biggest producer as well as consumer did not become a net importer until the 1940s.

## Cold War years

That shift occurred as the world moved into the Cold War era and oil quickly became embroiled. For the Cold War protagonists the national liberation struggles and the decolonisation process of the second half of the twentieth century were arenas of competition for influence. Simultaneously, the spread of oil nationalism – the assertion of control over national resources – from Latin America to the Middle East, Africa and Asia, introduced new players, the producer countries themselves. Their emergence at that time inevitably led to them being implicated, rightly or wrongly, in Cold War machinations. So, one of the founding fathers of OPEC, the Saudi Abdullah Tariki, was ludicrously nicknamed the Red Sheikh in the US and Europe.

A major concern of the US and Western Europe was that the Soviet Union, which became more than self-sufficient in oil and natural gas in the 1950s, would use exports as a strategic weapon. Another was that it would seek to constrain Western access to Middle Eastern oil.

One of the early battles of the Cold War was over Soviet attempts to gain access to Iranian oil resources at the end of the Second World War. The Soviet Union occupied part of northern Iran at the end of the war and hoped to secure political influence, further the longstanding Russian dream of access to a warm-water port, and obtain oil needed in the short term pending post-war reconstruction. The US strongly opposed this and demanded the withdrawal of Soviet troops. Moscow agreed to pull out in return for the establishment of a joint Iranian and Soviet oil company. The troops went, but the Iranian Majlis refused to set up the company. In Eastern Europe, Russian oil and natural gas assisted in the process of tying satellite economies to the Soviet Union.[6]

Elsewhere, the incorporation of oil at less than market prices and oil technology into trade deals provided Moscow with both foreign exchange and influence. So in the 1950s, although Washington persuaded the Bolivian government to drop a cooperation agreement between its state oil company and the Soviet Union, in 1959 Brazil agreed to take Russian crude into its refineries. Most famously, after the Cuban Revolution of 1959, Havana gained subsidised Russian oil in return for sugar, an arrangement that only ended with the collapse of the Soviet Union. Soviet oil engineers were active from India to Yemen to Ghana.

Washington urged its European allies to eschew offers of cheap Russian oil or at least to avoid long-term contracts. By the 1970s, as détente kicked in, the policy all but collapsed in Europe. Indeed, back in the 1950s, the decision of the Italian state energy corporation, ENI, to buy and market cheap Russian crude had helped to start a price war in which price cuts were imposed on Middle East producer countries, an event that stimulated the development of OPEC.

Russian self-sufficiency, for Washington and its allies, at least meant Moscow was less likely to attempt to seize a part of the Middle East for itself. But there were other concerns, most prominent being possible Soviet sponsorship of radical Arab movements and regimes. In the event, those movements and regimes probably proved far more adroit at playing the field than either Washington or Moscow expected. If they were happy to accept what Moscow would offer in return for a little ideological posturing, they also knew that they had to keep their main customers supplied.

Venn points to a divergence in European and US tactics in dealing with troublesome producer countries in the years after their independence and the ending of the old concessions. Britain and France proved intransigent and militaristic in their former colonial stamping grounds. Washington was for a long time unconvinced by London's complete rejection of Mussadeq's nationalisation of the Iranian oil industry, having learned to cope with a nationalisation in Mexico, and decided to refund its oil companies for the increased payments they had to make to the Venezuelan government rather than risk a confrontation that might drive Caracas in the same direction as Havana. An Arab critic of the regimes of the Middle East, writing about the 1930s, notes earlier expressions of this divergence:

> The differences between the consortia who subscribed to the colonial agreements and the Americans reflected their national character. The British companies were assumptive, directly dependent on the political muscle of their government to maintain concessions, allocate production and post prices. Arab leaders created by the colonialists and dependent on them for their very existence never questioned the companies' policies – no one dared. On the other hand, the Americans, unaccustomed to colonial behaviour and the resulting economic exploitation, 'cooperated' with the local chief, Ibn Saud. He was totally dependent on what they paid him, and they knew that 'the concession is always in jeopardy unless his (personal) demands are met'. The results were similar: the rulers were sustained in power by what the oil companies paid them.[7]

Then came the 1956 invasion of Egypt by Britain, France and Israel after Nasser's nationalisation of the Suez Canal, through which Europe received its supplies of Gulf crude. Washington opposed the move and forced a withdrawal, not least by refusing to supply Britain and France with crude when Egypt responded to the attack by blocking the canal.

Washington's preferred means of achieving its strategic objectives regarding oil was through oil companies. This was true in the Middle East and in the US's backyard of Latin America:

> In examining Venezuela in conjunction with Saudi Arabia we can discern certain similarities of treatment by the United States. Clearly demonstrated is the overriding importance of the oil industry in both countries, as American government and American companies alike acted to protect their investment less by outright obstructionism and

more by limited concessions.... What also emerges, however, is that while the State Department was willing to exercise pressure on behalf of its desired objectives, it still expected its oil policy to be conducted largely by the companies.[8]

However, by 1973, it appears US policy had taken on a far more militaristic aspect. Papers released by the British government in 2004 reveal concerns that Washington would invade Saudi Arabia, Kuwait and the UAE if the Arab oil embargo continued.

## Producers to the fore

In a document of the most highly secret classification – UK Eyes Alpha – circulated to the prime minister, a clutch of senior cabinet ministers and senior security agency staff, Percy Craddock, head of the intelligence assessment staff, drew on comments made by senior US diplomats suggesting that by December 1973 Washington could be preparing to intervene militarily in the Middle East.[9] The analysis presented is that in the case of protracted restrictions in oil supplies, perhaps because Arab–Israeli fighting flared up again, and a serious threat to Western economies, the US might decide to secure oil supplies. It assesses US, European and Japanese requirements for Arab oil at 760 million tonnes a year, a little less than the September 1973 output of Saudi Arabia, Kuwait, the UAE and Libya. As higher output could be achieved from the first three, action against geographically removed Libya is put to one side. It goes on to look at how the objective might be achieved, including 'replac[ing] the existing rulers ... with more amenable men', the use of Iran or Western European countries to do the job, threats of force, and blockades, but concludes that 'the American preference would be for a rapid operation conducted by themselves to seize the oilfields'. The areas seized would have to be held for some ten years, according to the document. A calculation of the initial and subsequent troop numbers needed and the logistical requirements follows.

In an indication that the optic through which energy security was viewed had already shifted from one of Cold War to one in which oil producers themselves were seen as a direct and primary threat, the paper argues that 'Russian intervention would probably stop short of direct military intervention' and that Washington would probably tip off Moscow beforehand. Then 'the Russians would try to make the greatest political and propaganda capital out of opposition'. The greatest danger of indirect Cold Warrior confrontation would be in Kuwait, if Russia encouraged Iraq to intervene there.

The paper is pervaded with an air of concern that Britain might be asked by its dominant ally to assist in an invasion. For by now Britain preferred to settle its oil-related problems diplomatically. A fortnight before the intelligence assessment was circulated, the prime minister and other senior members of government met with Sheikh Yamani, the Saudi oil minister, who spoke on behalf of all Arab oil producers.[10] Yamani not only stated that Britain was classified as a friendly country that would receive oil supplies in line with those before the embargo began but added he was willing to look at ways of compensating Britain for volumes it lost by being able to source oil from the Rotterdam spot market, a particular target of the embargo. France and Spain were also classified as friendly, while the rest of the then European Economic Community, except for the Netherlands, was judged neutral.

The events of 1973 comprise two separate strands that have too often become tangled. The issues of oil price, on the one hand, and control of reserves and manipulation of production for strategic purposes, on the other, are of course interlinked. However, their conflation results in the sloppy analysis served up by right-wing politicians in the US. It is also evident in the reductionist arguments of some opponents of the 1991 and 2003 wars against Iraq.

In the first years after it was established in 1960, OPEC's actions were largely defensive, an attempt to halt price reductions imposed by the producer companies rather than to increase them. A decade on, and Gulf producer country governments were receiving $1 a barrel for oil sold by the companies for $12–14 a barrel. At the same time, the real value of that $1 was being eroded by the growing weakness of the dollar. However, by 1970 a number of member countries had learned from founder member Venezuela and adopted its pricing legislation whereby the producer government received both royalties and taxes on oil. In 1971, OPEC succeeded for the first time in pushing the oil companies to negotiate with the organisation rather than individual countries. Moreover, through what became known as the Tehran Agreement they were able, collectively, to win increases in the 'posted' price hitherto set by the companies, and raise their tax take to 55 per cent. The Tehran Agreement also included an annual price escalator. Another important element was acceptance by the companies that the price should be protected against the falling value of the dollar. At the same time, member governments were moving towards the assertion of control over their reserves through the nationalisation of existing production. OPEC had agreed to pursue a policy of gradual nationalisation but some members moved ahead more quickly. Algeria nationalised 55 per cent of French interests, Iraq took control of IPC assets, Libya took over BP's operation. Saudi Arabia began an extended period of gradual nationalisation of Aramco in 1972.

By 1973 it was clear the Tehran Agreement would no longer hold. The price of oil sold on the open market was soaring and the producer countries demanded a share. Negotiations reopened in October but failed, leaving a group of Gulf producers to impose their own price increases. Open-market prices continued to soar, pushed higher by the embargo on sales to the US, the Netherlands and South Africa imposed by Arab producers in response to those countries' support for Israel during the October War, and in December a 140 per cent rise, taking Arabian Light crude's posted price to $10.84 a barrel, was dictated by OPEC. From this point on, Fadhil Al-Chalabi, a former senior OPEC official, wrote, 'Opec has been the sole price administrator.'[11] Al-Chalabi's point is correct to the extent that the companies and the consumer country governments with which they closely coordinated conceded they could no longer impose prices on producer-country governments. However, it would soon become clear that OPEC members' divergent interests would make collective price strategy difficult to achieve.

A minute of a UK government cabinet meeting dated 16 October 1973 demonstrates a high level of concern about OPEC's move to raise prices, quite separate from concerns raised by the Arab embargo, which was only due to be discussed in Kuwait the day after the minute was written. The prime minister informs the cabinet that the rise proposed would cost the EEC members an additional $10 billion a year. Incidentally, it also notes that the oil companies had consulted with ministers on tactics.[12]

While the campaign to push up posted prices to try to align them more with those on the open market was pursued by OPEC as a whole, the key members including Venezuela and Iran, the embargo action initiated on 17 October was taken by members of the Organisation of Arab Petroleum Exporting Countries. Its aim was to pressure the US into dropping or moderating its support for Israel, not to impact the market, although clearly the ministers who agreed the embargo would have understood the implications of their actions. This was the second use of the 'oil weapon', which was briefly and unsuccessfully wielded after the Six Day War of 1967 in which Israel invaded the West Bank and the Gaza Strip. Then, popular outrage and spontaneous action forced several Arab oil producers, including Saudi Arabia, into a short-term embargo of the US, Britain and West Germany, which failed because replacement crude was quickly sourced from the US and Latin America.

Interestingly, the 1973 UK cabinet minute cited above also deals with preparations for a possible embargo but makes no reference to prices in those paragraphs. Price negotiations and embargo were seen as separate issues. And, as Venn notes, one of the most hawkish countries on the price issue at the time was Iran, which was uninvolved in the embargo and a close ally of the US, while the linchpin of the embargo was Saudi Arabia, which was struggling in OPEC to moderate price demands.

Indeed, there is evidence that the US was supportive of OPEC's campaign to raise prices in the early 1970s. Pierre Terzian, in his history of OPEC, runs through a number of pieces of evidence suggesting the Nixon administration encouraged, even stimulated, OPEC members to push prices up believing it would help boost US production, disadvantage Japan and Europe in trade competition with the US, and create a market for US goods in oil-producing countries.[13] There was also the issue of maintaining friendly regimes. When prices were high, Secretary of State Henry Kissinger went on record warning that to bring them down aggressively would threaten the stability of important allies.[14]

There are two reasons why the US would opt for higher oil prices. First, staged, moderate increases in prices fitted with Washington's post-war policy of compromise rather than confrontation with producer country governments in both Latin America and the Middle East. As the volume of imports into the US rose inexorably, it became more and more evident that the country could no longer act as global 'swing producer' – the producer that increased or decreased its output to ensure a global balance between supply and demand. That role had now passed to Saudi Arabia and there it remains. The second reason is that US governments then and now have to bear in mind that their country may be a dominant importer and consumer but it is also a major producer. The US oil and natural gas industry provides income and employment for a vast number of voters, not just staff of household-name companies but a host of small independents and, indeed, 'mom and pop' single-well producers.

Low oil prices meant and still mean lower income for these US businesses, which form powerful lobby groups at the state and federal levels. And because the cost of production in the US is well above that of OPEC, the latter has a fatter cushion to absorb price falls. Price rises, on the other hand, might cost manufacturing industry but they also benefit the exploration and production sector, enabling continued investment. Without that investment, import dependency grows even faster. A high-level government–industry–academic seminar noted in 2003 that, for all the rhetoric,

> few market players would want to see a truly competitive environment emerge, as the resulting low prices would bankrupt all but the lowest cost producers, which are the Arabian Gulf countries, not the non-OPEC countries. Low prices will thus give more relative economic power, not less, to Middle Eastern oil producers.[15]

The divergence of interests between the oil producers of the US and the industrial and domestic consumer has traditionally been resolved by keeping taxes on oil and natural gas very low in comparison with Europe. The problem posed by OPEC's shift from the defensive to the offensive was political rather than economic at root. The effective assertion of collective petro-nationalism was not simply a matter of paying more for oil. Rather, it represented a loss of control over a vital natural resource. It also raised fears that other commodity producers might band together. Hitherto, it had been possible to ensure international commodity organisations comprised both consumers and producers, thus denying the latter the ability to exert their collective strength. In the event, this rather than the OPEC model was the one that prevailed, largely because tropical agricultural producers lacked the muscle of oil producers. Where the international commodity agreements did have price-influencing mechanisms, such as withholding schemes, by the 1990s they were abandoned.

The consumer countries, through their companies, had lost the power to determine that prices, be they rising or falling, were aligned to their broad economic needs. Henceforth, consumers would rely to a large extent on the unwillingness of OPEC members to kill the goose that laid the golden eggs by pushing prices so high that they choked off demand by damaging consumer country economies. Additionally, and worryingly given the volatility of the Middle East where the US blatantly sponsored and supported Zionist colonialism, the sidelining of the companies in price setting meant the US no longer had a cutout between itself and the producer countries. The linkage between oil issues and political issues was exposed. In both cases the US was on the other side of the table from the Arabs. As a history of the industrialised countries' International Energy Agency notes,

> it could not be excluded that the oil producing countries might also find that their oil wealth, then rapidly increasing in value, could be employed not only to economic advantage, but also as a weapon to obtain political objectives in wholly unrelated areas of international relations.[16]

The use of the embargo weapon was the logical expression of this. The embargo petered out in the new year, formally ended by Saudi Arabia in March.

# The IEA: meeting collective action with collective action

The Arab members of OPEC had cut production from 20.8 to 15.8 million barrels a day and announced they would not export to the US, the Netherlands (from which open-market oil was shipped to Israel), Portugal, Denmark, Rhodesia and South Africa. The cuts were to be increased each month. The impact on OECD country economies was considerable. US gross national product fell 6 per cent in 1973–75 and in 1974 Japan's GNP fell for the first time since the end of the Second World War.[17]

It was the use of the 'oil weapon' rather than OPEC's campaigning for higher prices that shook industrialised consumer countries out of what a number of observers have seen as complacency. The response was to meet collective action with collective action in the form of the International Energy Agency (IEA). The producer country cartel OPEC had been formed to confront the operator company cartel of the Seven Sisters, the powerful major oil companies whose dominance was eroded by the development of the independent oil companies and the state companies of producer nations. Now the IEA was created as a consumer front that would replace the companies as torchbearer of the industrialised countries, standing against 'a permanent organisation rapidly advancing to meet its aim ... ready, with well-developed economic and political resolve, to act in the future on behalf of producer countries'.[18] To date, no crisis addressed by the IEA has been caused by the OPEC bogeyman.

Hitherto, the major oil consumers of the West had only weak and rudimentary systems in place to cope with oil supply disruption, principally some agreed guidelines on apportionment of available supplies within OECD European countries, a recommendation that countries build up stocks equal to 90 days' consumption, and a cumbersome advisory structure that left decision-making power with the highest bodies of the OECD, which ruled on the basis of unanimity. In fact, in 1973 OECD Europe's stocks stood at just 70 days and the apportionment provisions were never used or their use proposed because it was known that unanimity could not be achieved.

The IEA, while still an arm of the OECD, and created by the bulk of the OECD's European members in alliance with the American members, the US and Canada, was crafted to respond to short-term emergencies while addressing longer-term issues of energy security. Japan was brought in but France maintained its Gaullist fiction of non-alignment and remained outside until after the 1991 Gulf War, even though the IEA's headquarters was in Paris. In contrast to the previous arrangement, IEA members would have a legal obligation to establish minimum supply levels – initially 60 days but soon raised to 90 – and the secretariat would have power to trigger an oil-sharing mechanism that would take the sting out of future embargoes or other disruptions affecting a subset of members. Systematic arrangements were put in place to gather information from the oil companies, which, in practice, would be responsible for holding some two-thirds of the stocks. Members were to have demand restraint plans in place.

The IEA was established to pre-empt and react to supply disruption, not to keep a cap on prices, although the two activities are closely related. To trigger the oil-sharing mechanism a 7 per cent shortfall of supplies for individual countries or the group of members was needed with stock releases and demand restraint measures available to cope with lesser shortfalls. Indeed there have been rows over just when the agency should intervene and it has criticised unilateral action by member countries – the US and Germany – when they have used stocks apparently to bring down domestic prices.

The 1973–74 embargo took something over 4 million barrels a day on average out of the market over its duration. The period November 1978 to April 1979 saw the biggest supply disruption so far experienced, with a gross 5.5 million barrels a day taken out of circulation – 10 per cent of global demand – as Iranian oil workers threw their weight behind the campaign to overthrow the shah. Prices soared to unprecedented heights and again OECD economies suffered.

By March 1979 the IEA judged supply disruption to be serious but not sufficient to trigger the sharing mechanism or coordinated release of stocks. Rather, it asked but did not instruct members to cut consumption by 5 per cent. A request by Sweden for activation of the oil-sharing trigger to help it out was declined; other ways of maintaining supplies to the country were found. A better-coordinated OECD was able to ride out 1978–79 even though oil prices did double to $25–30 a barrel.

The year 1980 brought a new disruption as Saddam Hussein launched an invasion of Iran, leading to a decade-long war of monstrously bloody proportions. Conflict around oil-producing areas and the Shatt-al-Arab waterway leading into the Gulf reduced Iraqi exports by 3 million barrels a day and Iranian exports by 1 million barrels a day. Again the IEA did not need to activate its emergency response, although members agreed on measures to cool the market, including urging companies to stay off the overheated spot market and draw down some of their very high level of stocks. This, combined with Saudi Arabia's customary willingness and capacity to make up for shortfalls, burgeoning North Sea production, and dipping consumption trends – in part due to recession and in part due to post-1973 energy efficiency measures – gradually rebalanced the market. There would be the so-called 'tanker war', attacks on offshore installations, and many more years of conflict between Iran and

Iraq but oil prices had reached the crest and were about to begin a long-term decline.

It was Saddam's next military blunder that provoked the IEA's only ever full response to supply disruption. The August 1990 invasion of Kuwait and subsequent UN boycott of Kuwaiti and Iraqi crude brought a gross loss of over 4 million barrels a day to the market. Prices roared up to over $40 a barrel on the spot market, but they were propelled by 'headline trading' rather than fundamentals. Indeed there was a modest stock build in the OECD, and the IEA reported the market well supplied, with Iran and Saudi Arabia pumping for all they were worth.[19] In fact, OPEC pleaded with the agency to moderate the markets, calling for a controlled release from record stockpiles.[20] On 11 January 1991 it was OPEC that declared it would supply a further 2.5 million barrels a day in the event of any supply shortfall. Only a week later did the IEA activate its Gulf War Contingency Response Plan, authorising the release of over 2 million barrels a day onto an already steeply falling market. The move came on the day military action against Iraq began. The reasons given for acting then were the contentious claims that Saudi Arabian production might be vulnerable during Operation Desert Storm and that the reaction of Arab oil producers was uncertain (notwithstanding the known incapacity of the Iraqi air force and the OPEC decision earlier in the month). In the event, only about half of the crude oil made available by the US and by Germany from stocks was actually bid for and in March the plan was deactivated. Scott remarks in his history of the IEA that 'The contrast between the foregoing levels of preparedness for the Gulf Crisis, and the inchoate measures and the disarray of the industrial countries in the period leading up to and during the 1973–74 crisis is quite remarkable.'[21] In among the self-congratulations of the Governing Board was a telling note of the important role played by oil producers, particularly Saudi Arabia and Venezuela, in mitigating the effects of the crisis.

The strategic shift towards coordination between the powerful consumer nations is credited with taking the sting out of the threat of major disruption to oil supplies, however caused. The power of the strategy to date has been in its potential rather than actual use, as has been seen. The threat of its use may have changed producers' behaviour, one argument being that Saudi Arabia's willingness to fill supply gaps over the past three decades has been driven by the kingdom's determination to ensure that it rather than consumer governments earn the profits from selling oil on the market. (The counter-argument is that Saudi Arabia has always been willing to pump more and moderate prices.) Within the US there is a debate over whether the country's Strategic Petroleum Reserve should be maintained as a political and strategic instrument or developed into a market management tool used to cap prices, rather in the way OPEC has developed in recent years a mechanism that triggers increases and decreases in production when prices fall outside a price band of $22–28 a barrel.

The 2003 invasion of Iraq by the US and UK again saw the IEA called upon to utter assurances that it was ready to act. Its new executive director, former French energy minister Claude Mandil, promised massive releases of oil if necessary. The agency released a fact sheet stating its members had stocks of 4 billion barrels, representing 114 days of net imports, and that publicly held stocks could be drawn down at a rate of 12.9 million barrels a day for the first month of a crisis.

In the event no action was needed. During the years of sanctions against Iraq since 1990, and the constant manoeuvring around the workings of the UN-operated oil-for-food export programme, the market had become accustomed to periods of withdrawal of Iraqi crude. Again, it was assurance from other OPEC members, particularly Saudi Arabia, that obviated the need for the IEA to do more than state its willingness to act. Mandil spoke to Saudi oil minister Ali al Naimi and to Qatari oil minister and OPEC president of the time Abdallah al Attiyah as the invasion of Iraq began. They 'gave me personally very strong comfort and some details of how they were producing and storing', he said.[22] The IEA stood ready to supplement producers' actions to keep the market supplied. This open acknowledgement of interaction rather than competition between the IEA and OPEC stands in contrast to the early years of the agency as expressed by the refusal of its second head, Helga Steeg, to allow the producers' organisation to be mentioned in agency publications.

## Garrisoning the Middle East

Since the IEA was established when energy security was viewed as a chess game between producer and consumer blocs, the Iranian Revolution, the Kuwait crisis and the invasion of Iraq had shown that crises were, in fact, generated by what Washington characterised as 'rogue states'. Whether or not active consideration was given by the US to invading Arab oilfields in 1973, a decade later the shift to US military activism in the Middle East was fact. As President Reagan went on a $1.7 trillion arms spending spree, part of the strategy comprised the Rapid Deployment Force, an army of 300,000 troops to be deployed rapidly via regional allies such as Morocco. The rhetoric of Reagan and his defense secretary Caspar Weinberger returned international relations to the wintry depths of the Cold War. The hand of Soviet interference was seen everywhere and the doctrine now was that

> It is essential that the Soviet Union be confronted with the prospect of a major conflict should it seek to reach oil resources of the Gulf. Because the Soviets might induce or exploit local political instabilities,

their forces could be extended into the area by means other than outright invasion. Whatever the circumstances, we should be prepared to introduce American forces directly into the region should it appear that the security of access to Persian Gulf oil is threatened.[23]

As a commentator of the time remarked, regimes of any political persuasion would have to continue to sell oil; the Soviet need for Gulf oil was entirely hypothetical; and furthermore the Soviet Union's need to import grain had not led it to invade Argentina. Rather,

> It would appear that the question of 'security access' amounts to the preservation of US energy companies' dominance of the processing and global marketing of Persian Gulf oil. For this, US military planners have, in effect, wired up the Saudi throne and those of the other ruling families in the area, to a nuclear tripwire.... In its present phase, Washington is promoting the nuclear arms race as the ultimate guarantor of the status quo.[24]

At the same time, the US was deepening its involvement in the Middle East and North Africa through indirect means: the traditional military, diplomatic and financial aid to Israel, propping up the Sadat regime in Egypt after its peace deal with Israel; arming former Soviet client Saddam in his war against Iran; imposing sanctions against Iran; and arming Morocco in its war against Algerian-supported Polisario fighters in the Western Sahara. By 1987 a Kuwaiti request for assistance against the threat of Iranian attacks on its oil tankers had provided a pretext for US naval deployment in the Gulf, a deployment that continues out of a base in Bahrain for the Fifth Fleet to this day.

By 1990, the Reaganite Cold War fig leaf for US military involvement in the Middle East had gone, as had the Soviet Union to all intents and purposes. But the abiding strategic interest in the region remained. As Joe Stork and Ann Lesch noted on the eve of Desert Storm,

What is at stake, in the view of many people in the Middle East, are four intersecting issues: (1) the legitimacy of the existing political and economic order in the region, which the US is striving to maintain and which Iraq appears to be challenging; (2) the control of the region's resources, especially oil, and the distribution of their proceeds; (3) the resolution of longstanding grievances, particularly the conflict between Israel, the Palestinians and the Arab states; and (4) rivalry among Arab states for dominance.[25]

They are right to put oil within a nexus of interlocking strategic issues and also to speak of 'control of' rather than access to oil, which has never been purposefully threatened except at the level of populist rhetoric outside of the short-run and very particular circumstances of 1973.

After the 1990–91 conflict in the Gulf, US forces in the Middle East were further built up at the invitation of local regimes concerned that they had stirred up the Iraqi hornet's nest. The range and number of US military facilities in the south-west Asia area is staggering. Excluding the major facilities in Turkey and those in North Africa, which fall under the US's European Command, US Central Command has bases or basing agreements in 11 Middle East countries plus 5 in Central Asia and 3 in the Horn of Africa. There are 25 primary deployment facilities, 40 logistics bases, and 14 training bases. In the middle of 2004, there were some 170,000 US troops in south-west Asia. Central Command also had some 17,000 air force personnel and around the same number of naval personnel. Then there were over 26,400 marines in Iraq and hundreds more in the Horn of Africa.[26]

There is every likelihood that substantial numbers of US troops will remain in Iraq and Afghanistan for many years. But even stripping out the troops in those theatres, the number of bases and other US facilities in the region means that the Middle East is hosting, willingly or unwillingly, tens of thousands of US military personnel, for example the 1,200 at the naval base in Bahrain and the 2,000 at the $1.5 billion Al Udeid air base in Oman, and was doing so long before the pre-Iraq invasion build-up.

US military spending has escalated in recent years. The cost of the 2003 invasion of Iraq to the US taxpayer is reckoned at some $150 billion, against $61 billion for the 1990–91 affair. In 2003 the military budget was some 15 per cent higher than the Cold War average. Military spending for 2005 is forecast at $400 billion.

## 'War on terror': new name, same policy

After the attacks on the US on 11 September 2001, energy security, in common with virtually every aspect of foreign policy and many aspects of domestic policy, were filtered through a new prism of 'terrorism'. The image that emerges often lacks resolution, as a contribution to congressional debate in the US from the senior Californian congressman Tom Lantos demonstrates:

> Until today, we have not examined how our reliance on Middle Eastern oil handicaps our ability to combat international terrorism.… America's dwindling oil reserves provide less than half of the oil our economy needs. This leaves us heavily dependent on the Middle Eastern regimes that control the vast majority of the world's known oil reserves. Many of these regimes are either actively hostile to the United States, as is the case with Iran, Iraq and Libya, or unsteady, autocratic regimes beholden to Islamic fundamentalists like Saudi Arabia.
>
> …many of these same regimes funnel oil revenues into support for global terrorist organisations. The Saudi royal family, for instance, pumps millions of dollars into radical religious schools and mosques across the Middle East…
>
> …our dependence on Middle East oil severely undermines our ability to combat international terrorism. Fearing another Arab embargo, some of our diplomats kowtow to Middle East autocrats and permit their anti-democratic, anti-American practices to go unanswered. It is distressing that US foreign policy in the Middle East is often held hostage to oil interests.[27]

With an outrageous conflation of regimes with organisations generally hostile to them and an absurd resurrection of the embargo bogeyman, Lantos's remarks exemplify the manner in which the events of September 11 were appropriated to bolster the case for war against Iraq and more expansive and deeper US intrusion into everything from regional relations in the Caucasus to shipping regulations. The testimony of Frank Gaffney, former assistant secretary of defense turned head of a security think-tank, was in much the same vein:

> I think it is clear our ability to wage effectively a global war on terror may be impinged upon, perhaps significantly so, if our enemies are able to disrupt or otherwise interfere with such energy flows.
>
> Secondly, we are in the bizarre situation of relying among the sources of Persian Gulf oil on Saddam Hussein, who President Bush has, I think, properly determined must be replaced.
>
> ...we are waging a war against those whose terrorist activities are made possible at least in part by the proceeds of American and Western oil purchases from the Persian Gulf. Specifically, such purchases are clearly enabling Saudi support for our Islamist enemies.[28]

The 'global war on terror' added impetus to longer-standing attempts to diversify US imports, particularly as the flow of oil from Canada slowed. In the National Energy Policy, published shortly after he came to power, George W. Bush's administration reiterated that, 'We need to strengthen our trade alliances, to deepen our dialogue with major oil producers, and to work for greater oil production in the Western hemisphere, Africa, the Caspian and other regions with abundant oil resources.'[29]

Lobby groups were quick to weigh in after September 11. In June 2002, the right-wing Institute for Advanced Strategic and Political Studies, an Israeli organisation that places researchers in both the Knesset and the US Congress, sponsored a press conference on Capitol Hill to 'discuss the strategic importance of West African oil to the US'. 'This initiative of IASPS is being furthered through the African Oil Initiative Group', according to the institute, which said that 'Saudi and Arab hegemony over US and world markets have been dealt a blow by the US intention to increase the African share of oil imports to 25 per cent by 2015.' Among the recommendations of the group are: that the Gulf of Guinea be declared an area of vital interest to the US; that a regional subcommand be established in the area; and that adversaries, including 'rogue' Arab states and 'US rivals such as China', be deterred from the area. By early 2004, the US army's European command had embarked on the Pan-Sahel Initiative, training troops from Mauritania, Chad, Niger and Mali, complementing the training and supplying of armies of the Maghreb. All this is part of a security strategy in the 'arc of instability' identified as running from the Caucasus, through the Caspian states, the Middle East and Sahel to the west coast of Africa. Virtually every country described by the arc is an oil or gas producer or a transit state or adjacent to such countries.

It would be wrong to confuse the recommendations of partisan lobby groups with actual or future geostrategic policy of the US or other powers. But what the recommendations do point up is the way in which the official rhetoric of free and transparent markets ensuring energy security is rapidly subverted by the quest for control over oil and natural gas reserves and transportation routes. And that brings with it more interventionism, more webs of alliances and enmities, and more potential flashpoints. Nowhere is this more apparent than in the Caspian Sea region.

## Securing the Caspian or opening Pandora's box?

The Caspian Sea region has long been one of great interest to foreign oil companies and governments, one of the jewels to be picked off the crumbling Soviet crown. Potential income to Western oil companies could reach $5–10 billion a year by 2010.[30] But the location of the oil and natural gas reserves means the manner of their exploitation is strategically sensitive to many players, including the states with a claim to reserves, potential and actual transit states, and potential customers. Much of the region formed part of the Soviet Union and before then a contested zone in the Great Game between European powers of the nineteenth and early twentieth centuries. It remains a region Moscow believes should be within its sphere of influence and so holds the potential for friction with Washington at exactly the time that the US is keen to access the Russian oil it boycotted in the days of the Soviet Union.

In principle, Western oil companies began gaining access to the oil and natural gas reserves in the early 1990s. In practice, developing them has been and remains a slow business. Notwithstanding constraints of technology and investment and the wrangle over the division of resources beneath the Caspian seabed, the primary issue has been how to transport oil out of the region.

Central Asia and the Caucasus remain highly unstable, as the collapse of Soviet-imposed borders and administrative divisions opens up a Pandora's box of issues around identity, ethnicity and nationality, combined with competition for access to available or potential wealth – wealth that is often rent associated with natural resource production or transportation. Recent conflicts include civil war in Tajikistan, the Georgia–Abkhazia conflict, insurrection in Azerbaijan, the Armenia–Azerbaijan conflict over Nagorno Karabakh, and the war in Chechnya. Additionally, there is internal instability caused by the incompetence and corruption of local regimes. In late 2003, the government of Georgia was overthrown by a popular uprising. Then there are dependencies inherited from integration into the Soviet Union, such as Russia's stranglehold over the Ukraine's access to European natural gas markets.

Just days after a new US–educated Georgian president was elected, US secretary of state Colin Powell flew in to demand that Russia withdraw its forces from the country. Georgia is a key transit country for Caspian oil. Moving on to Moscow, he emphasised that the US now sees the Caucasus as an area of strategic interest, challenging Russian policy in Chechnya and Moldova. Chechnya is a transit country for current, early flows of Caspian oil. A few weeks later Moscow retaliated, upping the ante with the threat of withdrawal from the Conventional Forces in Europe treaty. A power struggle then blew up between the new Georgian government and the pro-Moscow provincial government of Adzharia, leading Azerbaijan to warn of complications to the building of the Baku–Ceyhan pipeline and oil markets to worry over the 200,000 barrels a day of Central Asian oil exported through the Adzhari Black Sea port of Batumi.[31] As 2004 drew to a close, contested elections in Ukraine rapidly took on the complexion of a contest for influence between Moscow and Washington, threatening to tear the important transit country in two.

Meanwhile, the US had used the 'war on terror' as a pretext for building air bases in Uzbekistan and Kyrgyzstan while, of course, Afghanistan was occupied by US-led multinational forces in the wake of September 11. Indeed conspiracy theorists tied the overthrow of the Taliban government in Afghanistan to ambitions to build an oil pipeline through the north of Afghanistan into Pakistan, a project adopted in the 1990s by US oil company Unocal and recently dusted off.

The US campaign for control over Caspian reserves is most evident in its sponsorship of the Baku–Tbilisi–Ceyhan pipeline (BTC) as the main export route. Three routes were considered: west through Georgia and then on to the Turkish Mediterranean port of Ceyhan; west to the Georgian Black Sea port of Supsa, through the Bosporus into the Mediterranean; or south through

Iran to the Gulf. The Bosporus option was opposed by Turkey, partly because of legitimate fear of the dangers of increased tanker traffic through the heart of Istanbul, and partly because a pipeline through its territory presented much greater earnings opportunities for local construction companies.

The Iran option made plenty of sense. It was relatively cheap and easy to build and would bring earnings more quickly to the producer countries of the Caspian region. But Washington's antipathy towards Iran, exemplified in the 1996 Iran–Libya Sanctions Act, which threatened sanctions against even non-US companies investing in the Iranian oil and natural gas sector, led to the presidents of Azerbaijan, Kazakhstan and Turkmenistan being summoned to the White House in short order in 1997 and 1998 to be urged not to support the Iran option.[32]

That left the BTC option, carrying oil through Abkhazia and Nagorno Karabakh before reaching NATO ally but politically volatile Turkey. Persuading the oil company consortium to back BTC was made more difficult by the massive extra cost. In the end, the Turkish government had to stump up $2.4 billion of the cost, with the US providing a series of aid packages and grants to mitigate the cost. According to campaigners against the pipeline, Turkish government exemptions of the project from local law and assurances it would compensate the oil companies if laws were introduced that reduced BTC's profitability breach Ankara's accession agreements for future entry into the European Union.

Talking of the pipeline route issue, Alan Larson, an under-secretary at the US State Department said:

> one of the possible approaches would be to have that energy come primarily through Iran. There would be very serious and adverse consequences for us were that to happen, and that has been one of the reasons why the United States has worked very, very hard to provide the political foundation for the development of independent, multiple pipelines, including one that runs from Baku to Tbilisi to Ceyhan in

Turkey, because it is a way of assuring that that energy can get out and that it does not have to transit a country that might try to use its control over the transportation network as a source of leverage.[33]

But there is another reason for enforcing a westward flow of oil. Central Asian oil and natural gas are of great interest to China. A pipeline from the region to China will probably be built at some point but will be massively expensive and will take a long time to construct, not least because the industrialised zones of China where there is the demand are in the south whereas the pipeline would run in from the north. Executives of Petrokazakhstan, which produces oil from onshore Kazakh fields and sells small volumes into China, see little near-term prospect of building up eastward trade for exactly this reason.[34]

Yet Central Asian oil delivered into Iran could either be delivered to the Gulf for onshipment to China or other Asian markets or swapped for Iranian oil that would be transported to Asia, a practice already in place for small volumes of Kazakh and Turkmen crude. The US and European problem with this is that Central Asian oil would feed Asia – including China – whereas the routes into the Mediterranean 'turn Central Asian oil into European oil rather than Asian oil'.[35]

In its quest to improve its energy security by diversifying its oil imports, the US has immersed itself in the mire of instability in the Caucasus and Central Asia. A joint study of the issues by the Rand Corporation and the US Air Force is generally sceptical about the long-term importance of Caspian resources to US energy requirements and even more doubtful about US ability to force the resumption of oil flows if a state or states controlling pipelines stopped the flow. Turkey's cooperation through NATO would be needed, and the ability of Turkey and the willingness of NATO to become involved in military adventurism, particularly if it set them against Russia, is judged 'uncertain at best'.[36]

The risk of 'terrorist or subnational attacks' on pipelines and infrastructure is judged as posing a more difficult challenge. Pipelines are highly vulnerable to attack – there have been literally hundreds on Colombian pipelines in recent years, and US attempts to restart northern Iraqi exports after the 2003 invasion were dogged by unsophisticated sabotage attacks. Attacks on pumping stations or computerised control systems can cripple exports for months at a time. Natural gas pipelines are even more vulnerable because they require constant pressure.

In the past and in other parts of the world, oil companies have been able to make arrangements for the security of their infrastructure. In Nigeria, Shell controls a police force that it arms and that is supposed only to operate in specified areas. It was reported in 1996 that BP signed a three-year deal with the defence ministry to create a battalion of 650 men to defend its sites in Colombia. Two years later the company sacked a top security officer who had discussed arming the troops with attack helicopters and setting up psychological warfare operations.[37] In Iraq, 'private security' firms have been brought in to take over some installation protection duties from the occupying armies. Companies have benefited from cosy relations with the army in Burma and in Sudan. But these sorts of ad hoc arrangements hardly match the geostrategic challenges the US has taken on through its policy of seeking not simply to buy and import Caspian oil (probably from US-dominated consortia) but to control the whole process. This is a mission as dangerous and imperialistic as its attempts to impose its will on the Middle East.

### Targets galore

The mobility and unpredictability of the threat posed by unconventional forces came into sharp focus with the September 11 attacks on the US. The arrest in Morocco in June 2002 of a cell alleged to have planned to attack vessels in the Straits of Gibraltar, through which some 5,000 oil and oil-product tankers pass each year, followed by the holing with explosives of the oil tanker *Limburg* off the coast of Yemen a few months later, illustrated that the energy sector provided a wealth of potential targets.

Much attention was paid to US moves to enforce its security requirements on trade partners through its Container Security Initiative. In effect the US exported its line of defence against the use of container traffic to partner countries by saying that if requirements such as profiling and searching of cargoes and early provision of manifests were not carried out, traffic from non-compliant ports would face costly delays. In a number of ports, the US security regime has been exported in the form of squads of customs officers.

While shipping security concerns in the US have centred on the use of containers to transport men and materiel or act as delivery systems for dirty bombs, all other forms of commercial shipping have also been put under scrutiny. So, under strong US pressure the UN's International Maritime Organisation pushed through changes to legislation, putting in place a scale of security alerts for ports and new procedures and responsibilities for ship-owners and crews. The International Transport Workers' Federation quickly complained that it was its members who suffered immediately, being barred by armed US authorities from taking shore leave. Ironically, the ITF has long campaigned for an end to the 'flag of convenience' system, arguing that it was a means for unsavoury shipowners to disguise themselves while regimes such as that of Charles Taylor in Liberia could draw funding from the practice. The US and other OECD countries have been much less hurried in addressing this issue despite its obvious security implications.

The seaborne transport of oil and natural gas has come under scrutiny, of course. The threat of a vessel carrying hundreds of thousands or even millions of barrels of crude oil being hijacked or detonated in New York harbour or mid-way through Istanbul is the stuff of Hollywood thrillers, the consequences the stuff of horror films.

The tanker terminal of Valdez in Alaska, from which the US derives 17 per cent of its domestic oil supply, was closed in a security alert at the beginning of January 2004.

One of the first energy-related, post-September 11 security alerts was the denial of entry to Boston harbour of a Norwegian LNG carrier. According to some, attacks against LNG tankers and terminals could be particularly devastating as LNG fires only stop when all of the gas has been consumed, while oil and oil product fires tend to burn out more quickly.[38] Shell wheeled out a Nobel prizewinner in chemistry to downplay the danger, arguing that the force needed to puncture an LNG storage tank on a vessel or at a plant would be so great as to cause a localised fire rather than a far more widespread conflagration of leaked vapour.[39]

As demand builds inexorably and production diversifies, trade expands and with it the number and size of vessels carrying oil, oil products and liquefied (and condensed) natural gas. The IEA projects net interregional trade in crude oil to rise from 32 million barrels a day in 2000 to 42 million barrels a day in 2010 and 66 million barrels a day in 2030. Asian imports will rise almost fivefold to 24 million barrels a day by 2030.[40] The lesser inter-regional trade in oil products is also set to boom.

Interregional trade in LNG has been held back in the past by costs associated with the whole LNG chain, but with costs falling and demand rising, not least as previously self-sufficient OECD North America slips into a deficit that only LNG imports can address, the business will increase rapidly. LNG exports to North

America from Africa are seen rising from just 1.7 billion cubic metres a year in 2000 to a projected 97 billion in 2030, while those from the Middle East soar from 1.7 billion to 104 billion cubic metres.[41] Europe's dependency on imports grows similarly but will be satisfied to a large extent by natural gas imported by pipeline from Russia and North Africa.

The security and environmental issues raised by so great an increase in shipments of oil and processed natural gas are serious. Pipeline security has already been mentioned as an issue of geostrategic significance in the context of the Caspian region. The same is true of tanker shipping. The Malacca Straits between Malaysia and Indonesia are 2.5 kilometres wide. Some 600 vessels a day travel through the Straits, among them tankers carrying 50 per cent of Asian oil imports. Piracy is a major problem there. In 2003 there were 28 incidents of piracy in the straits. Worldwide, 23 per cent of the 445 reported acts of piracy were against tankers.[42]

In general, piracy against large vessels involves relatively petty crime – theft of stores, robbery of crew members, stealing fittings – and has been treated as a minor problem by shipowners. But the International Maritime Bureau, which monitors piracy, has noted a shift in trends where smaller vessels are concerned, with more activity by 'militia groups in politically vulnerable areas'. The stretch of the Malacca Straits bordered by Aceh, where separatists are fighting Indonesian troops, has been a particularly active area for piracy. IMB officials have also mentioned the possibility of a rise in the number of thefts of tugs and barges, vessels that could be used in attacks on larger ships.[43]

An increased concern over the possibility of attacks on shipping in bottlenecks such as the Malacca Straits, the Straits of Gibraltar, the Suez and Panama canals, the Arabian Gulf or the English Channel entail the upping of activity by the armed forces and

security services of local regimes. But, given the growing dependence of major consumer countries on energy imports, it probably
also heralds increased intervention by those countries in policing
shipping and in action against anti-government forces deemed to
be a potential threat to tanker traffic. It also heralds greater regional
tensions. For instance, China, with its growing dependence on oil
and LNG imports, worries about Indian maritime power.

It goes without saying that information-technology developments have been enormously useful for the energy industry,
enabling the rapid transfer of high volumes of data from site to
site, company to company. However, they have brought the threat
of new forms of espionage and sabotage, a threat that grows as
the technical competence needed to hack into systems becomes
more widespread. This is of increasing concern to both companies
and governments. As one security consultant observed: 'It is far
more likely that companies will be attacked by individuals who
are both educated and motivated by their cause. They will also
have the economic means to act and understand the consequences
of their actions.'[44]

## China: tomorrow's bogeyman

The likely next perceived threat to US energy security, the next
optic through which the world's most profligate user of oil and
natural gas will view the world, can already be divined. Increased
Chinese demand for oil and natural gas mirrors, indeed enables,
the country's rapid industrialisation and the growing strength of
its economy. One tendency in the OECD world is to view this
as an opportunity to recruit China into the ranks of organised
consumers, building up strategic reserves and pressuring producer
countries into moderating prices. But there is another view that
China should be considered a competitor for oil and natural gas

supplies. Exponents of this view are replacing the Soviet 'threat' with the Chinese 'threat'. Where Moscow was condemned for selling oil and arms cheap to buy political allegiance, China is alleged to be doing bilateral deals to obtain oil and natural gas. The expansion of Chinese oil companies into Sudan, Algeria, Gabon, and even in Saudi Arabia's upstream gas industry, is viewed with great suspicion. Thus:

> China has been willing to strike bilateral deals for oil with a number of countries, exchanging oil for what its counterpart seeks – which is often arms, missiles or nuclear technology. China's geopolitical strategy could well become a destabilising force unless it is more closely integrated within an international framework.[45]

Gaffney in his testimony to the House of Representatives committee began in measured tones but soon graduated to demonising China:

> if the Chinese economy achieves per capita energy consumption levels comparable to those of Japan … China alone would require some 70 per cent of the world's current oil production. Should, on the other hand, the Chinese reach contemporary American consumption levels … the People's Republic alone would require more than the entire global production of oil. This is obviously a formula for conflict with China, and, indeed, it is not surprising that the Chinese say, primarily for internal consumption, to be sure, that a conflict with the United States is inevitable, and I think they are preparing for that.
> … they are working assiduously to develop relationships with oil suppliers, most of them being what we call 'rogue states'…. They are trading oil for advanced weaponry, in some cases weapons of mass destruction-relevant technology.[46]

China is becoming an increasingly important player on the oil markets as its need for imports grows. The struggle to ensure Caspian oil goes west rather than south and east, to ensure it becomes European rather than Asian oil, has already been noted, as has the lobby group call to keep China out of Africa. A similar tussle is taking place in the Russian Far East, where two oil pipeline projects are competing. The cheaper would take up to 600,000 barrels a day of Russian oil into China. The more expensive would take up to 1 million barrels a day to the Pacific coast for shipment on to Japan. The choice is deeply political. At the domestic Russian level, it may be entangled with the Kremlin's spat with Mikhail Khodorkovsky, the head of Yukos, the major Russian oil company. But it has implications at the regional and international level as well. As a leading commentator on Russia put it, 'The Chinese pipeline is shorter and cheaper but places the destiny of Russian oil exports in the hands of the Chinese.'[47] That would be unwelcome to Tokyo, which needs to build and wants to diversify its imports. It would also be unwelcome to Washington, which is loath to see Sino–Russian relations become too friendly and which recognised in its national energy policy paper of 2001 that, 'In a global energy marketplace, US energy and economic security are directly linked not only to our domestic and international energy supplies but to those of our trading partners as well.'[48]

As a tanker broker remarked: 'Given declining Indonesian exports and limited growth for other Pacific basin exporters, China is becoming more dependent on Arabian Gulf and West African crude, which is good news for VLCC owners.'[49] This has not been lost on Saudi Arabia, whose relations with the US have grown increasingly strained since 2001. Ties between Beijing and Riyadh are on the rise, with Chinese ambitions of involvement in Saudi production rewarded in early 2004 with a deal with Chinese company Sinopec, alongside similar contracts with west European and Russian but not US companies. The Saudis will expect, in return, participation in China's downstream – refining and marketing – oil industry.

As one seasoned oil market watcher observed, the ascent of China as an importer gives Gulf producers a choice of who to deal with: 'It may well be worthwhile to both Arabs and Iranians, who together possess two-thirds of the world's known proven oil reserves, to take advantage of this new international power configuration. Make friends with China and make friends with India.'[50] The same commentary goes on to advise: 'Make new friends through trade. Take all of your eggs out of the US basket, and then use them to put pressure on America, instead of having America put pressure on you.'

## Security through diversification: chasing a chimera

In the wake of the 1973 oil embargo, US President Nixon unveiled Project Independence, which was to achieve US self-sufficiency in energy supply by 1980. (It soon became clear the objective was unattainable, so it was changed to a plan to maximise domestic supply and reliable foreign supplies at the minimum possible cost.) After the price rises of 1979, President Carter said 'it is essential that the nation reduce its dependence on imported fossil fuels' and put in place an ambitious set of policies to boost domestic production of hydrocarbon and alternative fuels. More than two decades later, President George W. Bush's Energy Policy Act of 2003 followed the well-trodden path, aspiring to 'to provide a comprehensive national energy policy that balances domestic energy production with conservation and efficiency efforts to enhance the security of the United States and decrease dependence on foreign sources of oil.'[51]

OECD countries did adjust their energy usage patterns as a result of the rising prices of the 1970s, in part due to energy efficiency measures and in part due to slower economic growth. Oil demand growth fell to 0.65 per cent a year between 1975 and 1985. US imports dropped from 7.3 million barrels a day in 1976 to 5 million barrels a day in 1980. With alternative sources of oil coming on stream, such as the North Sea, the percentage of US imports from OPEC members slid from 69.3 per cent in 1976 to 36.1 per cent in 1985. The percentage derived from countries of the Arabian Gulf had actually doubled to around 25 per cent between 1973 and 1976, notwithstanding the 1973 embargo, but after the Iranian Revolution it was trimmed right down to 6.1 per cent.[52]

However, as economic growth strengthened so the secular trend of higher imports reasserted itself and with it the importance of OPEC and the Gulf producers with their vast reserves and spare production capacity. In 1990, US imports hit the 8 million barrels a day mark, with OPEC providing 53.8 per cent and Gulf producers 24.5 per cent. By 2002, imports stood at 11.4 million barrels a day, 40.1 per cent from OPEC and 19.8 per cent from the Gulf. And, so much for a policy of reducing dependence on 'rogue states' – when Iraq was given clearance to export oil again in 1996 by the United Nations, the US quickly became its biggest customer, by 1999 importing 725,000 barrels a day, peaking at 795,000 barrels a day in 2001 and still running at a hefty 442,000 barrels a day in 2002 as Washington prepared to invade the country.

The policy of diversification of import sources may expand the reach of Washington's diplomatic and military assets but, as seen above, it necessarily also risks security flashpoints. Will it mean the US can escape the implications of projections for future oil supply sources? Can the Caspian, Russia and West Africa provide the US with enough oil to fulfil the four-decade-long quest to reduce import dependence on OPEC and the Middle East?

There has long been a suspicion that US administrations have exaggerated the potential of Caspian region reserves and the speed with which their exploitation could begin. The Rand

Corporation report cited elsewhere, albeit using estimates that have since been uprated, is sceptical about the overall importance of the region: 'From the West and Nato's perspective, therefore, while the emergence of the Caspian Sea region as an important source of global energy will contribute to improved energy security, Caspian energy supplies are unlikely to become critical to the West's security and prosperity, or a potential strategic vulner-ability.' And again, 'Notwithstanding much of the hyperbole that surrounds what has been written about Caspian oil, it is hard to escape the conclusion that the energy potential of the Caspian basin is of limited geostrategic significance.'[53] On the optimistic assumption that Azerbaijan and Kazakhstan were producing 3.5 million barrels a day by 2010, that would account for just 7 per cent of projected OECD demand.

Russian oil production and exports have been building steadily, breaking record after record. They are likely to continue to do so – one forecast is that exports will level off at 7 million barrels a day around 2010.[54] At the same time, natural gas exports will find growing markets in Asia and in Europe. ExxonMobil believes Russia will supply 40 per cent of Europe's additional gas demand. The UK and Russian governments have agreed in principle that Russian natural gas will mitigate the British deficit when the UK turns from net exporter to net importer as North Sea reserves are depleted. Western oil companies, from the minnows to the super majors, and financial institutions such as the European Bank for Reconstruction and Development, have moved in to develop everything from fields deemed too small to bother with by the privatised Russian industry to vast projects such as Sakhalin in the Far East. The US has made the strategic decision to begin importing Russian crude directly (some having found its way there via Venezuelan refineries in the 1970s), and in the summer of 2003 imported around 500,000 barrels a day. OECD Europe has long imported Russian crude and the volumes are growing, from around 2.7 million barrels a day in 2001 to over 3.4 million barrels a day in 2003.[55]

To make assumptions about the direction of Russian energy policy is risky. While the government is anxious to collect the rents from increased oil and natural gas exports, and the companies, domestic and foreign, are keen to earn the revenues from exports, the very centrality of the energy sector to the economy means it is contested. The speed at which export pipeline capacity is increased will determine the rate of export growth. Some analysts see export growth stalling in 2005–06 in the absence of new pipelines, and Russian officials have been quoted saying they do not believe Russian oil exports to the US will increase significantly until at least 2007 because of these constraints. LNG exports to the US are not expected before 2010.[56]

The government has held on to control of the major pipeline systems and this remains a crucial tool for controlling the privatised companies, with which the Putin administration has had a stormy relationship. The role of the state is a major area of dispute. Should the government reassert some control over the reserves Yeltsin sold off so cheaply? Should the companies be allowed to develop their own export pipeline networks or should the state maintain this lever? Should a national oil company be established?

Then there remain disagreements over the best models for integrating foreign capital into the industry. The government and parliament have fought long and hard over production-sharing-agreement legislation. Legislative and judicial uncertainty and dissatisfaction remain an obstacle to Western companies. Lee Raymond, chief executive of ExxonMobil, has called for a whole range of changes to Russian legislation, from a new law governing underground resources to clarifications of the tax regime to arbitration regulations.[57] In a country where popular sentiment remains firmly of the opinion that Russia's resources belong to the Russian people, all these issues are sensitive and have the capacity to ruin straight lines on graphs. Looming behind all of the unresolved issues is the big question of what political model Russia will finally adopt and how this will determine its partners in the energy sector.

The combined market implications of new Russian and Caspian oil are of concern to OPEC, according to one model implying either a fall of $1.50 a barrel in the price of OPEC crude for each additional 1 million barrels a day of exports from the Former Soviet Union, or a major cutback in OPEC output to defend the price.[58] Russia's relationship with OPEC is opportunistic. When world prices have slumped Russia has agreed cosmetic arrangements with OPEC to appear to be assisting in bolstering prices. But the reality is that Russia is a relatively low-cost producer intent on raising its market share and more than ready to undercut OPEC's target price range. However, a shift in political thinking in the Kremlin could change this.

The development of new oil supplies from West Africa has been based not on the political considerations that ruled the opening up of the Caspian and Russia to western oil companies and their governments but by technology. It is now possible to find and exploit commercially oil thousands of feet below the surface of the Atlantic ocean. The principal African producers of this deep-water crude for the foreseeable future will be Nigeria and Angola, but there is exploration and development work going on all the way up the west coast of the continent, and glances are now being cast towards East Africa. Angolan production is set to double to over 2 million barrels a day by 2008 as fields such as Kizomba, Plutonio and Dalia join Girassol.[59] All of these fields are operated by US and European oil companies and the high-quality oil is in strong demand all over the world. If planned projects all go ahead, West African production will rise from 3.5 million barrels a day in 2003 to around 6 million barrels a day in 2010.[60]

So, the Caspian, Russia and West Africa do have the potential to supply a much greater volume to world markets by the end of the decade, perhaps totalling 5–6 million barrels a day. And output is rising elsewhere – in Brazil, for example. But this has to be set against declines in the North Sea and the US and Canada, and global demand seen by the IEA rising to 88.8 million barrels a day, 13.8 million barrels a day above the 2000 figure. As noted in the chapter on supply and demand, world oil (and to a lesser extent natural gas) supply is set to grow increasingly dependent on OPEC's preponderant reserves, concentrated in the Middle East and North Africa and centred on the Arabian Gulf. The IEA sees OPEC members supplying 48.3 per cent of world oil in 2020, rising to 54.1 per cent in 2030, up from 38.4 per cent in 2000. Middle East members' share of the OPEC total will rise from 73 per cent in 2000 to 79 per cent in 2030. Other analysts see the same trends.[61]

Seen in this context, the diversification of import sources by the US (and other OECD consumer countries), even if it is successful in the face of the political, security, financial and logistical uncertainties, cannot ensure future security of supply, particularly in the face of growing demand from China (and India) and the geographical expansion of its oil interests. The only thing that can ensure supply is control over the heartland of OPEC.

## Controlling Iraq, replacing Saudi Arabia?

That is the background to the military intervention of the US and its allies in the Arabian Gulf. The arming of Iraq against Iran in the 1980s sought to contain a potentially troublesome regime in Tehran. As a US academic remarked in 1991:

Oil may not have been the only reason for US intervention in the Gulf but it was surely the primary reason. If not for oil, why would Iraq's aggression against Kuwait have been more important to the United States than Libya's aggression against Chad, or Syria's against Lebanon or Israel's aggression against Lebanon in the early 1980s?[62]

Alkadiri and Mohamedi of the Petroleum Finance Corporation in Washington are right when they stress the importance of control rather than the future role of US companies in Iraq: 'Without doubt, Washington does see a major role for foreign oil companies in the expansion of the Iraqi oil sector – a vision it shares with senior officials in the Iraqi oil ministry. But calculations about "controlling" Iraqi oil figured most.'[63] Privatisation and globalisation of the Iraqi energy sector are favoured means to an end but not the only means, and the end is control not contracts.

Prior to the 11 September 2001 attacks, US government policy appeared to have accepted that Saudi Arabia and other key Arab OPEC members could be relied on to ensure security of oil supply. The National Energy Policy welcomed moves by Algeria, Kuwait, Qatar, Saudi Arabia, the UAE and non-OPEC Oman and Yemen to open up to foreign investment in the sector and noted:

Saudi Arabia ... has been the linchpin of supply reliability to world oil markets. Saudi Arabia has pursued a policy of investing in spare oil production capacity, diversifying export routes to both of its coasts, and providing effective assurances that it will use its capacity to mitigate the impact of oil supply disruptions in any region.[64]

But the involvement of a number of Saudi nationals in the attacks, and reports and rumours of the complicity of figures within the Saudi establishment, jolted the belief that Riyadh's decades of partnership with Washington in keeping oil prices below the levels other producers would have liked could be relied upon. At the same time, resentment was growing over the stationing of US forces in the kingdom, particularly against a background of fierce confrontation between the Palestinians and the Israeli army.

Plans were announced to withdraw most US troops from Saudi Arabia in the hope that would both stabilise the kingdom and ensure US forces were out of harm's way. The new major air facility in the region was to be in Qatar, perhaps not unrelated to the tiny emirate's gargantuan natural gas reserves, some of which are intended to find their way to the US in liquefied form. Some have suggested that the decision to evacuate Saudi Arabia contributed to the decision to invade Iraq. They cite assistant secretary of defense Paul Wolfowitz saying that the repositioning of US forces was a major incentive to attack Iraq.[65]

A corollary of this argument is that if Saudi Arabia's vast reserves of oil could no longer be relied upon to damp prices, then Iraqi reserves could be if they were controlled by a partner or stooge. If Iraqi output flourished with international investment, then, in combination with increased Russian and Caspian flows, there would be a price squeeze that would set OPEC member against OPEC member in a struggle for market share, not for the first time.

Iraq had long been problematic, going back to its championing of the newly founded OPEC and its early steps towards nationalisation of concessions. Then, after a decade of support against Iran, it had invaded Kuwait (perhaps believing the US had signalled a lack of interest in the matter). Years of post-war sanctions had weakened the country's population, economy and the limited capacity of its armed forces but had left the regime unchallenged in any serious sense. And then Saddam had begun a rapprochement with Syria, beginning exports of oil to its neighbour and raising the spectre of a common approach to political issues of the region.

Throughout the years of the oil-for-food programme, the Iraqi government had played difficult, slowing and stopping exports for periods ranging from a few days to weeks, at one point helping to trigger a small release of strategic reserves in the US because of a spike in heating oil prices in the winter. The market learned how to cope without Iraqi oil and the impact of Baghdad's moves lessened over time, to the extent that rumours circulated that the primary reason the regime tried to move the market on occasion was to enable key members to make a killing buying and selling futures contracts. Moreover, to the extent that Baghdad could make promises for the day sanctions were lifted, it had made them to Russian, French and Chinese companies, awarding contracts or letters of intent for the development of massive oil fields, such as Majnoon, West Qurna and al-Ahdab.

All of this was grist to the ideological mill of the ascendant neo-conservative current in US Republicanism, championed by the likes of then national security adviser Condoleeza Rice and secretary of defense Donald Rumsfeld. Their argument and belief, in contrast to the more sophisticated view of Colin Powell, then secretary of state, was that Iraq presented a security threat to US interests in the region and one that should have been eliminated in 1991. An Iraq tied to the US would relieve the pressure on Israel and lead to pro-US governments being set up across the region. As Alkadiri and Mohamedi commented in another of their persuasive analyses:

> What they seem to anticipate is the emergence of a region much like Eastern Europe in the 1990s – where a benign group of democratic states is focused not on regional conflict and violence but on domestic reform and economic prosperity, and looks to the US for political and economic leadership.[66]

Subsequently, it emerged that a neo-conservative tendency in Washington was suggesting the Saudi regime be chastened by a threat to encourage and support the country's Shia minority to pursue secession, depriving Riyadh of oil and further cantonising the region while securing US access to hydrocarbon reserves.[67] The notion smacks of ignorance, foolhardiness and breathtaking arrogance, but so to many did the notion that invasion, occupation and privatisation would be welcomed by the people of Iraq.

# 4

# Petronationalism

The social and economic effects of oil on a nation state are often divisive and degenerative. Yet in the second half of the last century, oil was a medium of struggle to establish a degree of economic independence from the former colonial powers and US hegemony in Latin America.

In the 1970s, some oil producers briefly attempted to harness their improved market position to directly political ends through the Arab oil embargo, and there was an effort to force discussion of global economic inequality. These endeavours are popularly associated with OPEC, the Organisation of Petroleum Exporting Countries, which was formally inaugurated in 1960. In fact, OPEC has often been demonised for events not of its making. The embargo, as previously noted, was instituted by Arab oil producers, while the North–South dialogue was an initiative of OPEC and particularly Algeria, a leading light in the Non-Aligned Movement.

OPEC may have made wrong calls over the years, such as the disastrous decision to raise output only weeks before the Asian economic crash of late 1997. At times it may have been a political

bear pit – when ministers were kidnapped by the legendary
guerrilla Carlos in 1975, or when the Iranian minister's place at
a meeting was taken by a portrait as the man had been captured
by Iraqi troops, or when Iraq railed against Kuwait and pushed
for a rise in the 'reference price' just days before invading its
wealthy southern neighbour. But the organisation is in its fifth
decade, has survived countless forecasts of its demise, continues to
attract enormous press, industry and governmental attention and
has symbolised as no other international body has the attempts of
commodity producer countries to coordinate policy and influence
the rent they receive for their natural wealth.

In fact, OPEC's history is one of moderation, even conciliation,
towards the OECD consumer countries, although it is a matter of
debate whether that moderation derives from the nature of the
organisation or from the overbearing influence of Saudi Arabia or
from the difficulties of framing coherent policy from a membership with such divergent geographies and sociologies.

The notion that producer countries should control their own
oil reserves rather than accept the production levels and prices
decreed by foreign oil companies found its expression in Latin
America, an oil-producing region where the nation-state was
defined geographically and conceptually earlier than in the Middle
East or Africa. Terzian, in his excellent study of OPEC,[1] identi-
fies 1936 in Venezuela and Mexico as where it all began. An
oil workers' strike in Venezuela against the conditions imposed
by foreign oil companies kicked off a process that would lead
to government moves to appropriate some of the profits accruing to the companies, first by way of higher taxes and later by
nationalisation. But before nationalisation took place, Venezuela
was to suffer through competition from cheaper Middle East oil.
Terzian argues it was the experience of producer being played
off against producer that gave birth to the idea of OPEC. In

Mexico, with its long revolutionary tradition, a Supreme Court judgment in favour of oil workers' demands led more quickly to the nationalisation of the industry, as early as 1938.

By the 1950s there were stirrings in the Middle East, with the government of Mussadeq moving to nationalise the industry in Iran and Nasser nationalising the Suez Canal through which Gulf oil flowed west. Syria was to take control of the pipeline traversing its territory in 1966. The invasion of Egypt launched by Israel, the UK and France in 1956 resulted in the Arab oil embargo on Israel being extended for a while to parts of Western Europe, bringing short-term fuel rationing in places.

Mussadeq was ousted largely because of a boycott of Iranian oil instituted by the cartel of foreign companies and powerful consumer countries. It would be another decade before the development of a new generation of oil companies without access to the traditional concessions over oil-producing regions would create the space needed for a producer country to face down the Seven Sisters.

## OPEC: the producers stake their claim

OPEC's first years were marked by timidity as the organisation established itself. Oil was priced by the concessionary companies, which also determined the production level in each country. Al-Chalabi describes it as pricing system reduced 'to the level of plunder' and constituting 'a veritable subsidy for the economic growth of the industrialised countries'.[2] Although OPEC's first move on pricing was mild in form – to resolve that companies would not be allowed to cut or amend prices without consulting producer governments – Al-Chalabi says it was important in substance as 'the first event in the history of international economic relations to give a practical significance, albeit a limited one, to the concept of the inalienable right of the developing countries to sovereignty over their natural resources'. Moreover, OPEC made the point that collective action and solidarity between producers was crucial to asserting that right. OPEC stimulated the wider development of resource nationalism that fed into the politics of the movement for a New International Economic Order. Gradually the organisation's growing list of members – from five in 1960 to thirteen in 1973 – was able to equalise pricing systems to remove the oil companies' ability to undermine more assertive governments by sourcing crude from the more compliant.

Although currently not a major producer in OPEC terms, Libya played a vital role in 1970 when the newly installed, Nasser-inspired government demonstrated that it was possible to go on a price offensive. The industry in Libya was not based on concessions to a cartel of companies. Rather, some twenty companies operated there independently. The government demanded a cut in output and a higher take. The companies were picked off one by one and Libya established a higher price for its high-quality crude, compensation for earlier lower pricing, and acknowledgement of the principle of regular price reviews.

The lesson was learned, and later that year OPEC agreed to pursue collective price negotiations with the companies. The following year, an OPEC meeting in Tehran resolved that members would enforce new prices by legislation if necessary and that they would embargo recalcitrant companies. The subsequent Tehran Agreement with the companies demonstrated that in a period of fast-growing demand the producer countries could bargain with the companies on an equal basis. A new price structure intended to last for five years was put in place, raising the price of crude by some 45 cents a barrel, instituting a small annual price increase, reordering price differentials and abolishing some company price discounts. In fact, the growth of the spot market outside of the traditional system of fixed prices was already undermining the structure. As global demand rose and the US removed import quotas, so the companies increasingly were able to win far higher prices for crude on the spot market than the posted prices agreed with producers. At the same time, producers saw the value of their earnings fall along with the slide in the value of the dollar and then the removal of the dollar from the gold standard. The companies proved intransigent and, against the background of further price rises amid the October War in the Middle East, OPEC declared unilaterally a 70 per cent rise in prices to $5.11 for benchmark Arabian Light crude, a price that reflected those seen in the open market.

By December the Arab oil embargo of selected consumer countries had pushed spot prices higher on fear of shortages and OPEC made its headline move, pushing its prices up by 140 per cent. While that decision clearly reflected market conditions, Al-Chalabi points out that the rationale given was qualitatively different to that of a trader opportunistically raising his prices to those prevailing in the market. Rather it was based on calculations of the costs of alternative sources of energy, an altogether more sophisticated method that recognised the importance of oil to the global economy.

Indeed, when the next explosion of spot market prices took place during the Iranian Revolution, OPEC prices lagged far behind. Although this was due in part to the cumbersome nature of the organisation's decision-making process, it was largely because of Saudi Arabia's reticence about raising prices. In May 1979, the kingdom was abiding by a posted price of $14.50 while the companies were selling it on at $23–24 a barrel. While North Sea producers took the opportunity to raise their prices by over 10 per cent, official OPEC increases were just 5 per cent. Terzian records one of the consequences of the two-tier market – a massive increase in corruption on the most fantastic scale, particularly in Saudi Arabia where members of the elite sold on oil allocated to them ostensibly at the official price but with commissions and kickbacks of several more dollars per barrel.

> Even at the official level, this gap between Saudi prices and those of other producers represented a loss of over $23 billion over the period February 1979 to September 1981.... The loss to the Saudi treasury would be higher still if one reckoned in terms of spot market prices. In practice, it seems that a fair part of these billions of dollars ended up in the bank accounts of a handful of princes of the Saudi royal family and their intermediaries.[3]

OPEC's tussle with the companies over who would control pricing was consigned to the sidelines by the development of the spot market and the later rise in importance of the futures market. The organisation would not be the 'sole price administrator' seen by Al-Chalabi and nor would the companies be able to dictate prices, although both parties would be more or less influential depending on the conjunction of planets in the universe of market conditions at a given time.

But price control was not the only course followed by OPEC. Closely associated but more political was the push for direct participation in the exploitation of their own countries' resources or nationalisation. In 1968, OPEC proposed participation on an initial scale of 20 per cent, rising to 51 per cent, with compensation paid, and participation was the route taken by most Arabian Gulf countries – Iran and Iraq being the big exceptions. However, there was no single model. In Saudi Arabia the government bought itself a 25 per cent stake of Aramco, the consortium concessionaire of US companies Socal, Texaco, Exxon and Mobil, in 1973, acquiring with it the right to market a quantity of oil. The gradual takeover of Aramco was completed in 1980. Kuwait moved faster, quickly taking 60 per cent and avoiding any obligation to sell its portion of the crude to the companies. This latter point was important because it committed the government to establishing its own marketing organisation and becoming a real market player rather than owning oil in title but handing sales and marketing decisions straight back to the foreign oil companies. The UAE's policy was similar. Qatar took full control of oil operations on its territory but, again, by agreement.

In Iran the state oil company remained the legal owner of the oilfields even after the overthrow of Mussadeq, with the Western companies technically working as contractors. But although the companies were transformed into 'lifters', purchasers and marketers of Iranian crude under long-term contracts with discounts, government earnings were matched with those of countries that followed the participation route.

Although Nigeria nationalised BP's assets in 1979, participation is the dominant model there to this day. Around half of Nigeria's oil is produced by Shell Petroleum Development Company, operator of a joint venture in which the state oil company holds 55 per cent, Shell 30 per cent, Total 10 per cent and Agip 5 per cent.

Enforced nationalisation by OPEC members (Mexico, Bolivia, Peru and countries in the Soviet and Chinese orbits having moved earlier) began with Algeria, which, in 1967, took over the major part of production and marketing. Then Libya nationalised BP's assets. Iraq in 1972 took over the Iraq Petroleum Company in the north and later the Basrah Petroleum Company in the south. In Venezuela, where right-wing coups with a proclivity for deals with foreign oil companies had delayed nationalisation for decades, the move was finally made in 1974 albeit with the companies being given favourable lifting deals for the bulk of the country's crude.

The assertion by major producers not only of the right to the lion's share of earnings from their natural resources and to influence the price at which they were sold, but also of the right to make decisions on the rate of production and marketing did mark a major shift in the structure of the global oil markets. Today, 14 of the top 30 international oil companies ranked by output and reserves of oil and natural gas are 100 per cent state owned, with another 4 having majority state ownership.[4] They account for three of the top four – Saudi Aramco, Venezuela's PdVsa and the National Iranian Oil Company – ExxonMobil being the only non-state company.

This massive transfer of wealth from a handful of Western oil companies and the industrialised consumer countries can only be seen as more equitable than what went before. But what must not be forgotten is the limits of the achievement. A previous chapter has examined the appropriation of revenues, the dangers of conflict, the increased poverty, inequality and authoritarianism that accompany oil wealth. It should also be remembered that oil wealth has not been lost to the OECD countries, it has merely reached them by different routes, cycled in through arms purchases and bank loans rather than oil tankers. In 1974 windfall earnings had allowed OPEC members to build up vast surpluses. Yet their balance-of-payment surplus of $67 billion quickly turned to a deficit of $2 billion as they borrowed from European, US and Japanese banks, and bought and bought.[5] The funds put aside for a rainy day were invested in the OECD countries, by 1977 some $58 billion, or in European currencies, some $60 billion by the same date.[6] More narrowly, the national oil companies were of differing calibre. Turner produced a damning critique of the Nigerian National Petroleum Corporation's early years, depicting it as technologically impotent and reduced to a milch cow for the Western operating companies.[7] Lack of access to technology, particularly deep-water and LNG technology, has been a factor that, alongside the need for capital, has encouraged a reintroduction of outside companies into OPEC members' hydrocarbon industries.

## From bear pit to central bank

OPEC is too often characterised as a monolith. It is no such thing, and never has been. If it had been, it would have been far more influential. The market that its members attempt to tame even as they ride it is violent and predictable only in retrospect. Every decision taken by ministers at OPEC meetings bears scrutiny by game-theory analysts. What holds members together is the desire to maximise revenues and the belief that this can best be done by working in concert. Yet they are divided by many things. For those with smaller, higher-cost reserves there is the temptation to aim for higher prices – to make the most of a finite resource. For Saudi Arabia, above all, vast reserves and low costs have traditionally steered the kingdom to seek high volumes for itself and hence higher market share, at lower prices but with the long term in mind (though the weakness of the dollar and pressure on the kingdom's budget is raising suspicions that this fundamental premiss may be challenged).

For the members with larger populations there is the need to fight within OPEC for higher export quotas or shares of the overall output ceiling. This is the case with Nigeria, for example, which is also under pressure from oil company partners to push up production as new reserves are discovered offshore. On the basis of costs and reserves, Iraq would have been expected to adopt a similar policy to that of Saudi Arabia, yet through the 1980s it was a price hawk because it needed funds to prosecute its war against Iran.

The quota system has become synonymous with OPEC although it did not figure for the first two decades of the organisation's life after an attempt to institute quotas in 1964 failed. A view is taken on demand for OPEC oil and the total volume is then divided between members according to a formula that takes into account physical factors such as reserves and capacity and some social factors. Allocation is the subject of frequent wrangling. Saudi Arabia assumed most of Iraq's quota after the invasion of Kuwait, and Saddam's regime demanded it be returned to it while Saudi Arabia argued that increased demand made this unnecessary. The UAE and Kuwait watch each other closely to ensure the one is not making advances at the other's expense. Countries with major new finds – currently Nigeria and Algeria – argue for upward revision of their shares.

Quota discipline is closely watched by the markets as a sign of stress within OPEC agreements. If prices are high, some members can be expected to cheat to maximise income, but that of course helps to bring prices down. If prices are low, some may overproduce to compensate their treasuries for lower-than-forecast income, thus bringing prices yet lower. In the late 1990s, Venezuela shamelessly broke its quota allocation over a long period, attracting the wrath of other members while its oil minister called on his peers to institute 'a new market paradigm'. This apparently meant a closer relationship with consumers, particularly the US in Venezuela's case, and was part and parcel of a drive to open Venezuela up to foreign oil companies again and possibly lead to a privatisation of the state oil company.

Particularly before the price crash of late 1997 the diversity of demands by members and the need to find compromises to ensure consensus meant frequent fudges and commercial decisions tainted by political considerations. As forecasting the oil market is anyway more of an art than a science, the scope for disaster is considerable, as the ministers' meeting in Jakarta in late 1997 demonstrated. Quotas were raised just weeks before the Asian economic bubble burst. Demand plummeted, followed by prices that eventually reached twelve-year lows of, in some cases, under $10 a barrel.

Eventually, producers re-established their grip, but it was not OPEC as such that did so. Leading members Saudi Arabia and Venezuela, which had been in a fierce fight for the US market, came together with non-member Mexico (another major exporter to the US) to announce a major cut in output to stabilise prices. (They came to an agreement among themselves over access to the US market.) This deal they took to OPEC and rammed through promises of cuts by the organisation's members. Additionally, they roped in cooperation from Norway, a clutch of smaller Arab producers and, in theory at any rate, Russia.

Out of this came a new, more managerial and less politically driven OPEC. Far from the rhetoric of redistribution of wealth between developed and developing worlds that characterised the Algiers summit of 1975, now the organisation was to work like a central bank, establishing a price band that if exceeded would trigger output increases and if undershot would bring cuts.

That Saudi Arabia was a prime mover of the 1999 recovery expresses a basic truth about OPEC: the massive importance of Saudi Arabia. The kingdom with its enormous reserves, low cost base, and policy of maintaining large spare capacity, has often acted as the 'swing producer' within OPEC, which in turn is the swing producer for the global market, adjusting output up and down according to demand. During the 1991 and 2003 conflicts in the Gulf, Riyadh assured the consumer countries it would and could compensate for shortfall in supply from Iraq.

Exactly because of the long life and low cost of its reserves, Saudi Arabia has been a proponent of lower prices than those favoured by many, often most, other members. This policy has dovetailed with the kingdom's close strategic relationship with the West, in particular with the US, a point acknowledged by the US administration and the IEA alike. Indeed the kingdom has in the past deliberately flooded the market with its oil in order to force other members to accept lower prices than they wished.

Moderation in pricing and depoliticisation of oil are the hallmarks of the Gulf Cooperation Council oil producers. One commentator observed: 'Since the GCC's establishment in 1981, regardless of the perceived provocation and antagonism by various western countries' foreign policies ... none of the GCC countries has "used" the "oil weapon".'[8] He went on to cite the clamour for the Gulf producers to react to Israel's 1982 invasion of Lebanon and revelations that the US was arming Iran (as well as Iraq) in 1986 as examples of provocation to which the GCC members did not react.

Predictions of the demise of OPEC have been almost perennial since the early years. Every disagreement and every price fall brings new forecasts of collapse or of shrinkage into a Gulf Arab producer group. Terzian notes them, and reporters covering OPEC conferences today are still required to trot them out. After the 1997–98 price slump, Morse wrote: 'Resource nationalism has practically disappeared from the discourse of international relations, and along with its decline has come the demise of the once-vaunted Opec.'[9] Five years later, journalists continued to flock to OPEC meetings. Wire, newspaper, radio and television reports carried forecasts of the outcome of meetings and oil prices moved on unexpected outcomes.

A look at long-run real crude prices puts the achievements of OPEC into context. The price hikes of 1973–74 took Gulf crude up to around $10 a barrel but since then, excluding the 1978–84 period, no further progress has been made and, indeed, long years have been spent defending the early achievements. The jury is out on whether the higher prices of 2003–04 signify a fundamental shift. Some oil companies began raising the price assumptions they use to justify projects, a signal of confidence that prices would remain higher. But while OPEC members enjoyed and took advantage of a period of higher prices to replenish their coffers, by early 2004 they were doing all they could to lower prices that remained stubbornly high.

OPEC policy and practice are of immense importance to the oil market, given the scale of its reserves and production. However, the market is much more complex now than it was in the early days of the organisation. The wild cards of political unrest in this or that oil-producing region have always been in the pack, as has the frequent divergence of interest between members. But new cards have been introduced – new producing regions, alternative fuels for power generation, coordination of consumer reserves policy, and highly volatile trading in futures and options as well as the physical spot market. Prices are now driven by and capable of reacting to a range of factors that can trump the policies of producer or consumer governments. That the price increases of the early 1970s have stuck but not been bettered can be characterised as a sign of OPEC's abiding strength or weakness.

The resource nationalism of the 1960s and 1970s may no longer exist within OPEC but that is because the organisation, for all its weaknesses and failings, has moved with the times, or, more pertinently, with the markets. Having asserted a degree of influence over the market, OPEC has struggled to manage it. But whatever the stresses on the group's unity, its survival, let alone its regular if not constant ability to coordinate massive changes in production and so influence prices, demonstrates its relevance to its members. Eleven major oil producers centred on the Arabian Gulf, but with others from North and West Africa, Asia and Latin America, find more benefit in membership than non-membership and all submit to a greater or lesser extent to its discipline. That said, OPEC has failed to attract new, large producers into its ranks, even if Angola is considering membership and Mexico has shown itself willing to cooperate. And just as Gabon and Ecuador left the organisation – the small scale of their output making them out of place in a body dominated by big producers – so Indonesia's membership looks anachronistic as its oil exports fall away.

## Return of the companies

The increasing importance of natural gas and the ongoing challenge of providing investment to maintain and expand hydrocarbon output have brought a rethink of the nationalism of the 1960s and 1970s, and Morse is right to point that out. So, has the increasing need to attract foreign investment diluted the independence of OPEC members' oil industries? And why is there no Organisation of Gas Exporting Countries?

The George W. Bush administration's energy policy document lists Algeria, Kuwait, Qatar, Saudi Arabia and the UAE as now welcoming international investment (as well as non-OPEC Yemen and Oman). It fails to mention that Iran, Libya, Sudan and Iraq have also long been open to Western investment in their oil and natural gas industries but have been under sanctions. In the first three instances those sanctions have been US-imposed. In the case of Iraq they derive from the UN, but this did not prevent French, Russian and Chinese companies from making provisional deals with the regime. Unilateral US sanctions against oil-producing countries have been unpopular with US oil companies and may have influenced the decision to reach an accommodation with Libya in late 2003, but their existence demonstrates again that simple corporate profit-seeking does not drive energy policy in the US even if it strongly influences it.

The reopening or proposed reopening of reserves to external companies has taken different forms in different countries. In

Iran it has harked back to the pre-revolutionary days when oil companies worked as privileged contractors. In Saudi Arabia, there remains steadfast refusal to open up oil reserves, but upstream natural gas is being made available. In Venezuela, heavy oil reserves were the first to be offered to outside investors. In Nigeria, where foreign companies had remained important as joint-venture partners and operators, deep offshore prospects and the growth of international demand for liquefied natural gas gave foreign companies the opportunity to increase their involvement. In Iraq the Saddam Hussein regime offered particular fields for development. By what means a new Iraqi administration will allow entry by foreign companies is not yet clear, but it is worth recalling Peter Odell's remark of some thirty-five years' standing that the official US belief is that 'only American companies operating overseas can ensure the continuity of supplies to the United States!'[10]

Clearly, the terms on which foreign oil companies invest in OPEC countries varies from country to country and project to project. Negotiations over rates of return in Iran have dragged on for years in some cases. In the Saudi natural gas agreements, Saudi Aramco retains only a 20 per cent stake and the foreign consortia also operate the fields.[11] But what is clear is that the countries need the investment, and the companies want the oil and natural gas, but only while it is cheaper to produce than it would be elsewhere. What is happening is no return to the concessions era but it is a dilution of national control over resources and it underlines the failure of producer states either to master new technologies or to build the financial reserves needed to develop their lifeblood industry. One consequence has been pressure from companies on Nigeria and Algeria to open up the question of quota allocation within OPEC, arguing that newly discovered reserves should not be restrained by current allocations. More dramatically, there are predictions that if the companies can successfully establish a grip on the Iraqi oil sector, they will be able to influence that pivotal founder member of OPEC towards eroding the organisation's key function of defending prices through production changes. Such predictions are likely fanciful but nonetheless represent an aspiration of the US right.

The reintroduction of foreign capital has not been uncontroversial. In Saudi Arabia it is reported that the oil minister was unenthusiastic about bringing in the companies, and early plans that would have allowed them access to the downstream natural gas sector were thrown out. Foreign access to Saudi oil production remains unthinkable. In Kuwait, plans to open up some oilfields to foreign companies have been opposed long and hard in parliament. In Venezuela, populist president Hugo Chavez reversed the trend towards privatisation and re-emphasised petronationalism and adherence to OPEC's principle of collective action. In Nigeria, popular dislike of the oil companies thrives in the producing areas. Calls continue for 'indigenisation' of the industry and a greater role for the handful of small, local independent oil companies. But the potency of such calls is dulled by previous failures and by suspicions that local companies are just another vehicle for self-enrichment by the elite. Moves to privatise the oil refineries were met with industrial action. In Iraq, the US-appointed governing council ducked out of talks with potential foreign investors in the oil sector on the grounds they should be conducted by a proper sovereign government, thus delaying plans to boost production to at least 5 million barrels a day by 2010, an ambition only achievable through production-sharing agreements or other arrangements with foreign oil companies.[12]

It is worth looking briefly at the production-sharing agreement (PSA) as a method of arranging the exploitation of oil and natural gas. The PSA was first developed by Indonesia in the 1960s as a way of replacing concessions while maintaining foreign investment. It differs from the Anglo-Saxon legal model, which is based on royalties and taxes and allows ownership of resources to be transferred to and between individuals and companies. The PSA is rooted in Napoleonic law, retaining the state's title to resources and, formally, permitting only the state to develop them, albeit usually through a foreign company or consortium. The model has the advantage that the government can argue it has not relinquished sovereignty and so protect itself from accusations it has sold off the family silver. The contracted company or companies also operate at sole risk and expense, while the state owns any oil or natural gas that is discovered. The reward for the non-state players is that they are allowed to recover capital and operating costs from production and receive a pre-agreed portion of further production – so-called 'profit oil', which may then be taxed – the rest being taken by the state. According to one account, some 45 per cent of countries operated a PSA system by 2003.[13]

However, the producer country's take from PSAs varies enormously. Indonesian PSAs give as much as 85 per cent of oil and natural gas to the government. With Western companies clamouring for access to Russia, the PSA covering Sakhalin awards up to 70 per cent of production above a certain level to the federal government. But for countries yet to demonstrate they have commercial reserves or that are in other ways too weak to bargain with potential investors the take can be far smaller. For Angola, the government's take is in the high teens of percentages in the cost-recovery phase. In Yemen, Canada's Transglobe Energy and its partners on Block 32 take 71 per cent of oil in the cost recovery period and 40.5 per cent thereafter. Mauritania's first oil development, the deep-water Chinguetti field, will yield the government just 13 per cent of oil for the cost-recovery period, rising to 25–30 per cent thereafter.

While PSAs do have attractions for host governments, their disadvantages are also recognised in the industry as including a generally lower level of revenue to government, and that only well into the future. The case-by-case negotiation of agreements is also seen as offering more opportunity for corruption. Nonetheless, their proponents argue that Russia's freeze on PSAs has stalled tens of billions of dollars' worth of investment and helped to limit foreign direct investment in Russia to only a fraction of that in China.

Royalty and tax systems also reflect (and alter) the relative desirability of a given oil or natural gas province and the strength of the players in a negotiation. So, the company EnCana, another Canadian, which produces around 20 per cent of Ecuador's crude, let it be known in late 2003 that it and a group of other companies considered royalties too high and had told the government it would not participate in future upstream developments if they were not lowered.[14] On the other hand, increasing confidence, and increasing revenues from growing oil output, has allowed Kazakhstan to toughen its terms and indulge in what one report termed 'economic nationalism'. There are proposals for a 50 per cent limit on foreign ownership of ventures, removal of tax stability, plus a new escalator tax based on oil prices.[15]

## An OPEC for natural gas producers?

Changes in the structure of the oil market stimulated the creation of OPEC, its apparent supremacy in the 1970s, its collapse into infighting and near irrelevance for part of the 1980s and 1990s, its resurgence after 1999, and the forecast of increased importance of its membership in coming years. Dependence on external financing and technologies to develop members' reserves further have also moulded and diluted the ethos of self-sufficiency and petronationalism of earlier years. It is too early in the development of global markets for natural gas, whether transported by pipeline or as LNG, to tell whether conditions suitable for an Organisation of Natural Gas Exporting Countries will arise. However, it is worth considering briefly the arguments against and for.

Natural gas is not sold on any one basis. In some parts of the world its price is indexed to oil, against which it competes in some applications, and alongside which it is often produced. In other places, such as the US and, arguably, the UK, it is a completely separate market. LNG pricing is seen by some industry players as remaining variable, sometimes priced against other projects, sometimes against piped natural gas, sometimes against oil or coal, and sometimes inflation-indexed. This variation is facilitated by the fact that much natural gas has been 'stranded'. That is to say it is located too far from a potential market. That was the reason given for decades for the vast and environmentally ruinous 'flaring' of natural gas produced with oil in Nigeria, for example. In these circumstances, the market has been led by consumers rather than suppliers. The issue has been which potential supplier would a potential customer choose to go to. 'Market access not supply of gas is what counts', according to one senior executive. The cost of the infrastructure needed for liquefaction, transportation and regasification has been prohibitive for developing country producers, forcing them to rely on foreign investors, who then own and control the business.

The received wisdom is that natural gas supply requires long-term contracts, and certainly it does from the point of view of the investor paying for a transnational or transcontinental pipeline. Executives at British Gas, a leader in the Atlantic Basin LNG trade, believe long-term contracts will predominate. There will be an increase in the number of short-term deals and some more selling of individual or 'spot' cargoes, but in essence the market is less 'liquid' than that for oil, they argue. Then there is the geographical and social diversity of suppliers and potential suppliers of the burgeoning LNG trade, from Indonesia to Equatorial Guinea, Egypt to Australia, Trinidad to Nigeria, Malaysia to Qatar, Iran to Algeria.

To sum up, those who do not foresee a cartel of natural-gas producers believe that conditions create a tighter bond between producer country and consumer or intermediary than between producers. But, as we have seen, demand for natural gas is growing rapidly. LNG import terminal projects are mushrooming in the US, and import projects of natural gas and LNG are ongoing in Europe too. Consumption in developing and OECD Asia is also on the rise. At the same time, development costs are falling fast. According to Malcolm Brinded, group managing director of Shell, Atlantic Basin LNG from Venezuela or Nigeria is now no more expensive to produce than natural gas produced by conventional drilling in the US and is cheaper than supplies piped in from Alaska. LNG plant costs have fallen by two-thirds in thirty years and long-distance delivery costs have been cut by half since 1990.[16]

As to the development of sales outside of long-term contracts, which was a crucial factor in OPEC members' ability and resolve to enter the market in their own right rather than accept low prices imposed by the oil majors, two things should be remembered. First, although the oil market is now largely driven by the futures and spot markets, the bulk of the world's oil is still bought and sold on a longer-term contractual basis. Second, the forecast scale of spot LNG trade is actually quite large. Shell's Brinded sees it reaching 10 per cent of the total. The president of Petronas, the Malaysian national oil and natural gas company, believes spot and traded cargoes will account for 30 per cent of the total.[17]

It is conceivable that just as rising demand for oil, followed by the development of a spot market with prices higher than posted prices, created the conditions for a shift in the balance of power from oil companies to producer countries, similar processes will do the same in the LNG market. The growing number of supplier and recipient terminals could also bring greater opportunities to erode the dominance of long-term contracts, particularly with lower transportation costs. For piped natural gas there is obviously not the same physical flexibility – a ship can change direction but a pipeline cannot – but the development of trading hubs and growing contractual sophistication make it possible to carry out complex swaps and other deals. As consumers will seek to establish a diversity of supply for reasons of energy security, LNG and piped natural gas will increasingly compete with each other, bringing their prices closer together and further increasing the liquidity of the natural gas market as a whole. Also, even leaving aside any political impetus to nationalise assets, falling infrastructure costs could increase the ability of local companies, state or privately owned, to take large stakes in future projects or buy out foreign players in existing projects.

The Gas Exporting Countries Forum was established in May 2001, grouping Algeria, Bolivia, Brunei, Iran, Indonesia, Libya, Nigeria, Oman, Qatar, Russia and Venezuela. The communiqués of the body are full of pious yet vague phrases about 'jointly searching for concrete and innovative solutions' and 'optimal utilisation of … natural resources' and the mutual interests of producers and consumers. Nonetheless, it is worth bearing in mind that member countries control some 66 per cent of proven natural gas reserves,[18] that they include seven countries with the experience of OPEC membership, and that the GECF is a producer countries' body dominated by developing countries. Even without Russia, which accounts for almost half of the group's aggregate reserves, and which currently looks an unlikely candidate for membership of an organisation comparable to OPEC, the forum has the basis for a powerful producer lobby or even cartel. It should not be forgotten that OPEC's first decade was one of timidity and confidence-building.

## Rise of the new consumers

Energy security has long been a facet of foreign policy and geo-strategic thinking in the industrialised countries, as we have seen. Now as major developing countries become major consumers of oil and natural gas, their governments and national companies too are embarking on an energy foreign policy. This, it will be recalled, is already causing concern in US political circles to the extent that it seems competition with China is becoming a major focus of energy policy. Whereas petronationalism of developing countries has been associated with producers, increasingly it will be associated with developing countries that are net consumers such as China, India and South Africa and/or have expertise and political reputations they can profit from, such as Malaysia.

The issues facing the Chinese are complex and various.[19] By 2020, imports will be two to three times higher than domestic production and 90 per cent will come from the Arabian Gulf. This will make it harder and harder to shelter the economy from the roller-coaster oil market. While political factors such as countering US influence in Central Asia by developing ties with the states in that region and with Russia, as well as winning the loyalty of the Uighuir regions, militate towards developing domestic production in western China, the economics do not stack up. Projects to develop closer energy ties with Kazakhstan and Russia in the late 1990s were thrown off course. At the geopolitical level, links with Russia and access to Russian oil and gas are influenced by mutual fear and rivalry between Moscow and Beijing.

China has not, so far, been able to tap into Central Asian or Russian oil and natural gas to a substantial degree. The direct flow of oil from Kazakhstan to China is minimal, and the future of a planned Russian Far East to China oil pipeline depends on Kremlin politics, as previously mentioned. The US and its European allies have so far ensured that Caspian oil flows west rather than east or south. Indeed, oil produced at a western Kazakhstan field in which the China National Petroleum Corporation (CNPC) has a majority stake is sold overseas, not to China. Attempts by Chinese oil companies to buy British Gas's stake in the North Caspian Sea consortium failed when existing (Western) partners pre-empted the Chinese bid.

Even if moves into Central Asia have had limited success to date, Chinese oil companies are now active in many parts of the world, trying to bolster overseas exploration and production as domestic demand rises. In 2002 CNPC was engaged in thirty projects, upstream and downstream, in the Middle East, North Africa, Russia and South America, Southeast Asia, as well as Central Asia. Over 140 teams were working in over forty countries, providing services.

CNPC and Sinopec now have oil-producing operations in Peru and Ecuador and show signs of wanting to expand. China was expected to take a 70 per cent stake in a plant producing the bitumen-based generating fuel Orimulsion in Venezuela and showed interest in bidding to produce natural gas in Mexico.[20] In Indonesia, another Chinese corporation, CNOOC, raised its stake in the Tangguh natural gas project to 17 per cent, making it the second largest partner after the operator, BP.[21] In February 2004, the Chinese president visited Gabon in West Africa and signed a deal with Total Gabon under which China would import Gabonese crude for the first time.[22]

The previous month Saudi Arabia gave Washington pause for thought when it finally awarded rejigged natural-gas exploration and production contracts for three zones. ChevronTexaco had bid for all three contract areas but won nothing, meaning US companies won nothing. Sinopec and CNPC each bid for all three areas, indicating a very strong level of Chinese interest, and came away with one award for Sinopec. The other awards went to Lukoil of Russia and ENI of Italy working with Repsol of Spain. Pundits were soon mulling whether the awards were sending political messages.

In the spring of 2004, Sinopec was reported to be in talks with Iran to import LNG in a deal that would also give the Chinese company access to upstream oil and natural gas reserves in Iran. In Sudan, China, India and Malaysia have cornered oil production, moving into the country in the wake of US sanctions and the retreat of North American and European companies like Talisman, OMV and Lundin as war raged and pressure from human rights groups built.

CNPC has a 40 per cent stake in the Greater Nile Consortium that produced all of Sudan's 330,000 barrels a day in 2003. That output was set to double by 2005 with CNPC bringing on production from Block 6 in 2004 and its joint venture with Petronas of Malaysia and ONGC of India coming onstream the next year. More exploration work was expected to bring more finds on those blocks. CNPC also planned to invest $150 million towards an expansion of the refinery it built at Khartoum in 1997 in partnership with the Sudanese government, and to build a new 750 km pipeline.[23] CNPC has invested more money in Sudan than in any other country.

Malaysia's Petronas has become an important player in international oil and natural gas exploration and production with interests in some twenty-four countries and pipeline and downstream projects elsewhere, including an LNG import terminal in the UK. Like CNPC, Petronas has a major and expanding role in Sudan, anchored in a 30 per cent stake in the Greater Nile Consortium. And, like CNPC, Petronas has no compunction about working in Burma, another country where Western companies have come under pressure from human rights campaigners to withdraw. There it has a large stake in the Yetagun natural gas development. It is developing expertise in deep-water work, participating in projects offshore Angola and Mauritania, for example. It also has a part of the high-profile Sirri oilfield and South Pars natural gas field projects in Iran. In Africa, Petronas took a stake in Energy Africa, a South African company that seeks to use its nationality as a key to participation in projects in the continent. International reserves in 2003 rose 25 per cent to 4.76 billion barrels of oil equivalent, or nearly 20 per cent of total company reserves, as the company expanded. International production, dominated by operations in Sudan and Iran, were some 240,000 barrels of oil equivalent a day.[24]

India's oil minister said late in 2003 that his country was to invest another $750 million in Sudan, participating in the new pipeline and the refinery expansion through state-owned ONGC. The company had previously announced it would take a stake of around 25 per cent in blocks 5A and 5B on the front line of the war as Austria's OMV sold up. Earlier it had bought out Talisman's 25 per cent stake in the Greater Nile Consortium. (Recently, the wave of Asian interest in Sudan was augmented by Pakistan's Zaver Petroleum, which gained an exploration block in Khartoum province.) ONGC has invested over $3 billion in overseas assets. The jewel in the crown is a 20 per cent, $1.7 billion stake in the Sakhalin-1 project in the Russian Far East. It has found a niche working in or reaching agreements with those countries – including Iran, Iraq, Syria and Libya, as well as Sudan and Burma – that Western governments have dissuaded the companies over which they have jurisdiction from entering. The company aims to produce over 400,000 barrels a day from overseas operations by 2010 and three times that by 2025.[25]

Energy Africa is an altogether smaller proposition but is interesting because it is a South African company that has shown a commitment to working on the continent. With roots in the apartheid-era Engen it has turned its nationality – once a guarantee of pariah status – to its advantage, marketing itself as an African company. From a production base of just 5,000 barrels a day in 1995 from UK North Sea assets, it has expanded to 22,000 barrels a day in 2003, around 16,000 barrels a day of which is produced in Africa, principally Gabon and Equatorial Guinea. It has assets in eight African countries outside of South Africa.[26] Energy Africa was, effectively, controlled by Petronas, which owned 8.7 per cent of the company directly and 80 per cent of Engen, which in turn owned over half of Energy Africa. In the spring of 2004, Tullow, an Irish-based, London-listed independent producer with long-standing interests in Africa, acquired Energy Africa.

None of these companies' overseas operations is in the first division of international exploration and production yet, but they are increasingly big players. Petrochina is ranked number 10 on operational criteria in the survey already quoted. Petronas comes in at number 19 and Sinopec at number 26, for example. The close relationship between the Chinese companies, Petronas, and ONGC and the governments of their home countries demonstrates a clear intent to further national as well as corporate interests by gaining direct access to oil and natural gas and so reducing dependence on the open market. Often they have sought out niches that Western companies were withdrawing from, were encouraged to avoid, or did not believe to be sufficiently rewarding. But increasingly the skills they are developing are allowing them to participate in prestige projects such as Sakhalin and South Pars.

Their strategy is in contrast to that of the state-owned companies of OPEC members, which have had domestic reserves enough to keep them out of the international exploration and production scene. Where the latter have expanded it has tended to be downstream to secure markets rather than in overseas upstream ventures. The strategy of the likes of CNPC and ONGC makes good business sense and leverages political connections and sympathies.

# 5

## 'Alternatives' to oil:
## environmental and 'security' imperatives

In March 1967 the *Torrey Canyon* spilled 31 million barrels of oil off the Cornish coast of England. The rocks and beaches of that prime fishing and tourist region and the coastline of Normandy in France were devastated. Television pictures of the time showed many Europeans for the first time one of the perils of their dependence on oil: seas thick with crude; wildlife smothered, choked and poisoned to death; livelihoods wrecked. Twenty-two years later and it was the turn of North Americans as the *Exxon Valdez* spilled hundreds of thousands of barrels of crude and 1,300 miles of pristine coast were polluted. In November 2002, the *Prestige* split and sank off north-western Spain. She was carrying some half a million barrels of fuel oil, much of which washed up along 200 miles of Galician coast. That disaster was another nail in the coffin of the local fishing industry.

A decade before the *Prestige* went down, footage from Kuwait of blazing wellheads and skies darkened by plumes of black smoke as Iraqi troops sabotaged installations as they retreated was another reminder of the polluting qualities of oil for anyone in the rich, high-energy-consuming countries who failed to notice the smog hanging over their towns and cities on a sunny day.

For many communities in oil- and natural-gas-producing countries of the developing world, the consequences of production of oil and its cleaner cousin natural gas have been a constant companion. The World Bank has estimated there are 300 major spills of oil a year in the Rivers and Delta states of Nigeria. In the same country almost 90 per cent of the natural gas produced alongside oil has been flared for decades, burned off into the atmosphere at the rate of some 80 billion cubic feet a year.[1] Only as commercial interest in the liquefied natural gas market grew and the possibility of finding small natural gas markets in the West African countries was identified were projects to use Nigerian natural gas developed. Flaring near to settlements has meant that some communities have not had a dark night for years. The rain is acidic and crops and animal life are destroyed.

Throughout the world, production projects and pipeline projects impinge on native peoples and their lands, from the Caucasus to the Arctic Circle, from the forests of Latin America to those of Central Africa. Years of campaigning by local people and by their allies abroad have highlighted the double standards often applied by oil companies and financial institutions, which are far more likely to demand environmental and social mitigation efforts in, say, the North Sea or Alaska than in a remote district of a developing country far away. This means that projects such as the Baku–Tbilisi–Ceyhan pipeline or the Chad–Cameroon production and pipeline projects have been far more closely scrutinised than their predecessors.

In 1995 the UN's Intergovernmental Panel on Climate Change (IPCC) reached a historic consensus that the climate of the world was changing, that a global warming phenomenon could be identified and measured, and that human activity was influencing the change in the world's climate. The IPCC consensus confirmed what many environmentalists had argued for years: that carbon dioxide emissions from fossil-fuel-based energy use were inseparably linked to changes that will have profound and devastating consequences for the environment. It seemed that no longer could the negatives associated with oil and natural gas be limited to the particular and contingent incidents or company practices that could be mitigated by codes of practice, pollution clean-up funds, environmental audits and so forth. Now it seemed inescapable that fundamental questions about energy sourcing and usage would be addressed. Yet political and commercial imperatives have prevented the IPCC consensus from being replicated in government and industry circles.

Some oil companies have chosen to hedge their bets and diversify into renewable forms of energy such as solar power. Shell will spend $1 billion on developing a solar energy business between 1998 and 2006. BP rebranded itself as an energy company and adopted a new logo to match. In earlier years they and others had diversified into coal to ensure they had the energy market covered. Others fought tooth and nail against acceptance of the evidence. Exxon, later ExxonMobil, held out against the weight of scientific evidence. The company, which one set of studies[2] calculated had alone accounted for 5 per cent of global carbon dioxide emissions since 1882 and in 2002 had produced hydrocarbons nearly equivalent to twice the total UK carbon dioxide emissions for the year, actively lobbied against the Kyoto Protocol process (see below).

An IPCC report of 2001 is clear that the build-up of the 'greenhouse gases' – carbon dioxide, methane, nitrous oxide and troposphere ozone – that cause global warming 'reached their highest recorded levels in the 1990s, primarily due to the combustion of fossil fuels, agriculture, and land-use changes.' Carbon dioxide is the main greenhouse gas and increasing concentrations are 'virtually certain to be mainly due to fossil fuel emissions'.[3]

Three-quarters of man-made carbon dioxide emissions result from fossil fuel burning. Much of the rest is due to deforestation. In 2000, 76.8 per cent of emissions from fossil fuel burning was accounted for by oil and coal, with gas fuels accounting for 19.3 per cent. Cement production and natural gas flaring made up the balance.[4]

Among the findings the IPCC describes as 'robust' are: that global temperatures in the twenty-first century are rising at rates unprecedented in 10,000 years; that nearly all land areas are likely to warm; that a rise in the sea level will continue for further centuries; that many areas will have more rain and in much more intense bursts but that increased summer drying over most mid-latitude continental interiors will increase the risk of drought; that some ecosystems and species will be irreversibly damaged or lost; that plant productivity in most regions will decline; that the impact of storms on coastal areas will be exacerbated by sea level rise.

Local political structures and their relationship with the OECD consumer countries determine who gets which benefits and disbenefits from oil and natural gas output in producer countries. The distribution of the consequences of global warming can also be seen through the lens of the political economy. Mirroring the difference in consumption patterns between the developing world and the industrialised world, in 2001 carbon dioxide emissions from US use of oil was between six and seven times that of the whole of Africa, for natural gas at least ten times (for coal around 5.5 times). The comparison between Western Europe and Africa is scarcely less marked. At the same time, fast industrialising economies such as China and India were major sources of carbon dioxide emissions. China in 2000 was the world's second biggest source of emissions. In part this is due to the relocation by OECD countries of their manufacturing capability to developing countries where labour and materials are cheaper. At the same time China has reduced its ratio of carbon dioxide emissions to output through a shift away from coal. Its ratio of carbon dioxide to GDP output fell by a dramatic 50 per cent between 1990 and 2001.[5]

The social impact of climate change is global. The low-lying Netherlands' exposure to coastal flooding and storm damage and its dependence on coastal defences is epitomised in the folkloric tale of the boy who blocked a hole in a dyke with his finger. A recent study commissioned in the UK noted that eastern England should be planning for an increase in heat-related deaths and illnesses, incidence of food poisoning and skin cancer, significant pressure on already overburdened water resources, new agricultural pests, changes to rail and road specifications, a greater number of extreme weather events.[6]

Yet if the impact is global, that does not mean it is evenly spread or that developing countries are as able to cope with or mitigate the effects. Among the extreme examples are some low-lying island nations such as the Maldives, which could entirely disappear as sea levels rise. Bangladesh already suffers severe flooding that has cost many thousands of lives. This will increase year on year because even if all fossil fuel burning stopped today, sea-level rise, once started, will not cease for centuries.

Global impact projections and scenarios are constantly being commissioned and reworked. One relatively early forecast was for a 90 million tonne shortfall of food by 2050, putting 30 million people at risk of starvation with 66 million facing 'water stress' while 20 million more would be at risk of flooding.[7] The suffering induced by global warming will be felt most immediately and most directly by those who have done least to contribute to it, many of them among the estimated 2.4 billion who rely for fuel on wood, dung and agricultural waste and 1.6 billion who lack access to electricity. The IPCC found:

> The impacts of climate change will fall disproportionately upon developing countries and the poor persons within all countries, and thereby exacerbate inequities in health status and access to adequate food, clean water, and other resources....Overall, climate change is projected to increase threats to human health, particularly in lower income populations, predominantly within tropical/subtropical countries.[8]

The financial services industry has been reworking its numbers since the early 1990s as insurance companies review the premiums they charge and the incidents they agree to cover. One of the world's largest insurers, Munich Re, has estimated worldwide damage from climate change at \$300 billion by 2050.[9] Some individual disasters could exceed the \$100 billion mark and annual losses are projected to reach \$150 billion within the next decade.[10]

## Kyoto: up to the top of the hill (and down again)

In December 1997 the international community responded to climate change by adopting the Kyoto Protocol to the UN Framework Convention on Climate Change. The document contained legally binding emissions reduction targets for developed countries – the ones responsible for the vast majority of historic and current emissions. By ratifying the agreement, the developed countries would commit themselves to cutting their collective emissions to at least 5 per cent under the actual figures for 1990 or 20 per cent under the projected emissions for 2010 were no action taken. The target was to be achieved by 2008–12. The cuts required of individual countries varied, so the US would cut by 7 per cent, Japan 6 per cent, while the EU would allocate cuts totalling 8 per cent among its members. Russia and Ukraine would only have to stabilise emissions because the post–Soviet collapse meant their economic activity in the late 1990s was far lower than the 1990 level and this was mirrored by the scale of greenhouse gas emissions. Some relatively low energy-consuming developed countries like Australia and Norway would be allowed to increase their emissions.

The Kyoto Protocol contained many compromises, such as the inclusion of emissions trading whereby developed countries could trade pollution permits among themselves or offset parts of their reductions by financing certain kinds of project in developing countries. There was also contention over the treatment of 'carbon sinks'. Forests recycle carbon dioxide and deforestation adds to global warming. Some corporations lobbied for afforestation projects to count against reduction targets. Nonetheless, in the face of concerted lobbying against the whole Kyoto process by major business interests, the Protocol represented a major symbolic victory.

Yet symbolic the Protocol long remained. In March 1998 it was opened for signature, ready to enter into force ninety days after ratification by at least fifty-five countries, including developed countries representing at least 55 per cent of 1990 global carbon dioxide emissions. Six years later it still had to accrue enough signatures from developed countries. The EU ratified quickly, but the George W. Bush administration steadfastly refused and the issue became a political football in Russia. By January 2004, countries representing 44.2 per cent of developed country emissions had ratified.[11] It was not until late 2004 that Russia, as part of a broader deal with the EU, agreed to ratify. The most modest of starts on the long climb towards a reduction in damage to the global environment was delayed until February 2005.

The Kyoto Protocol was negotiated on the back of a previous failure of developed countries to meet previous non-binding commitments to cut back to 1990 emission levels by 2000. By 2004, the chances of meeting Kyoto targets looked increasingly slim even with the requisite ratifications. A long and highly detailed study by the IEA of energy use in member countries over the previous thirty years found:

> The developments during the 1990s paint a gloomy picture of the prospects of reducing $CO_2$ emissions to the levels called for by the Kyoto targets by 2010. With few exceptions, emissions will have to be reduced at significantly higher rates than have been seen in previous periods.[12]

In the period 1998–2001 – that is, after the negotiation of the Kyoto Protocol – there was no overall progress in emission reductions even though many countries had initiated policies designed to achieve this. Indeed, in the EU the growth in emissions was higher than in the previous eight years.

The IEA mapped emissions and economic performance through the 1973–98 period and found that 'economic growth is the primary driver behind increases in energy-related $CO_2$ emissions'.[13] In his foreword to the report, IEA chief Claude Mandil argues that 'This shows that the oil price shocks in the 1970s and the resulting energy policies did considerably more to control growth in energy demand and $CO_2$ emissions than the energy efficiency and climate policies implemented in the 1990s.' Odell takes the link between economics and consumption even further back, arguing that Roosevelt's imposition of oil import quotas on the US in 1959 pushed costs up to $3 a barrel from $1.50, reducing consumption by 100 million imperial tons a year.[14]

## The cost of cleaning up emissions

The energy policies of the 1970s referred to by Mandil were driven by the rise in oil prices following the loss of consumer-country oil companies' control over pricing and the subsequent surges triggered by the 1973 Middle East war and then the Iranian Revolution in 1978. The efforts by the US and its allies to assert strong influence, control even, over the Middle East and other oil-producing regions is not without cost, and some critics of US energy policy, including some environmentalists, attempt to bolster a compelling scientific case for combating global warming with economistic claims. These have two strands, at least. One is to point out that projected costs of implementation of greenhouse gas reductions are not so enormous. Another is to identify the externalities associated with securing oil supplies.

The IPCC collated nine studies and found they forecast reduction in GDP for developed countries in 2010 of between 0.2 per cent and 2.0 per cent if the Kyoto deal was implemented without emissions trading. With full emissions trading mechanisms in place, the figures could be halved. Assuming a 0.5 per cent reduction, the implied cost to developed countries would be $125 billion or about $125 per person per year by 2010. For most economies in transition the effect would be negligible to positive.[15]

Eric Ash of the Royal Society, one of the authors of a distinguished report on economic instruments and emissions reduction, drew together a larger pool of reports costing much more radical cuts in carbon dioxide than those proposed by the Kyoto Protocol. These suggested that the effect of a 25 per cent cut in emissions on US GDP would range from a fall of 2 per cent to a rise of 2 per cent. For a 90 per cent abatement, the projections ranged from a fall of 1 per cent to a fall of 4 per cent. As Ash has commented, with a trend increase of 2 per cent a year for GDP, the price of a 90 per cent reduction in carbon dioxide emissions would be no more than 'the loss of two years worth of the increase in our affluence'.[16] Such cuts would be implemented through technology such as post-combustion 'scrubbing' of emissions from power stations and injection of $CO_2$ into underground reservoirs.

Arguing that the costs of ensuring supply of oil should be notionally added to the market price of a barrel in order to calculate a 'real' cost of oil opens up other paths. One leads in the direction of saying the higher 'real' cost of oil should be offset against the projected costs of reducing greenhouse gas emissions. From there it can be argued that the development and production costs of 'greener' energy sources can also be offset against the savings. However, the same pricing methodology could be used to justify exploitation of high-cost oil and natural gas reserves in OECD countries or alternative oil production systems like coal tar sands or gas-to-liquids technology, which would not represent any breakthrough in emissions control.

Estimates of the military and foreign aid costs supposedly associated with ensuring the Arabian Gulf can be relied on to continue the flow of oil to the major consumer countries vary dramatically. One study in 1990, when Saudi oil was selling at around $15 a barrel, argued that another $60 a barrel should be added to give the real cost to the US.[17] More recently, the director of the Earth Institute at Colombia University reckoned:

> The dollar costs of US military operations in the Middle East attributable to policing the energy flows are tens of billions a year, if not $100 billion or more. This amounts to a hidden subsidy to oil use of $10 or more per barrel exported from the region.[18]

The variation in cost estimates illustrates the problem of buying too much into an economistic discourse. The price of Middle East oil is an important but subsidiary and contingent issue to a wider set of US policies including geostrategic control over the Gulf, support for Israel, and imposition of markets 'free' enough to enable full US penetration. Furthermore, the argument might have purchase in the US where oil products are only lightly taxed but in Europe, where tax on petrol amounts to some two-thirds of the pump price, the argument can be made that government is already recouping the hidden costs of hydrocarbons.

## War gaming meets global warming

Ironically, perhaps, there are signs that it is the US military and security apparatus that could push the White House into reassessing energy and environment policy. The environmentalist discourse and the military planner's world-view come together in scenario planning. Where the environmentalist sees increased risk of drought, low crop yields, populations displaced by flooding, altered disease vectors, species extinction, the military strategist sees political instability, conflict over water resources, mass migration, competition for food – all of them threats to the global order. Since the 2001 attacks, the US military has become increasingly concerned about an arc of instability reaching from the Caucasus, through Central Asia, down into the Middle East and across the Sahel to the west coast of Africa, each country in the arc either a major oil and natural gas exporter or adjacent to one, or a transit country. Each country is viewed as susceptible to radical Islamism. But if to the existing poverty and repression is added further immiseration caused by global warming, then current plans to implant military bases or expand training for local forces through programmes like the Pan-Sahel Initiative appear puny.

In February 2004, a British newspaper[19] said it had obtained a suppressed Pentagon report opining that climate change over the next two decades could result in wars and natural disaster costing millions of lives. Climate change 'should be elevated beyond a scientific debate to a US national security concern', the report was cited as saying. According to the newspaper, the assessment of the speed and severity of global warming in the report is far more serious than even environmental campaigners had predicted. Bangladesh could become virtually uninhabitable; India and Indonesia could be torn apart by civil conflict; large parts of the Netherlands would be flooded; major conflicts could develop around access to the Nile, the Danube and the Amazon. In such conditions, richer regions would become fortresses against would-be migrants, the nuclear arms race would speed up as larger developing and newly industrialised countries sought to ensure access to resources – 'once again warfare would define human life'.

That the Pentagon is willing to consider such a scenario was seen as encouraging to the extent that by tying climate change to the military and economic security issues that have traditionally driven energy policy, either a change in policy by George W. Bush or new policy from a successor might result. Less encouraging is that if the thrust of the report were accepted, given the decades and even centuries needed to stabilise the atmosphere and slow down the climatic changes set in motion, those countries that can afford to do so could be expected to put major effort into increasing their military and security assets. In other words a new long-term policy enlightened by self-interest would be accompanied by an even greater short-term concentration on military intervention, albeit conceivably accompanied by humanitarian palliatives.

## 'Alternatives': blurring security and sustainability

The terms 'alternative fuels' and 'energy conservation' are associated in much of the world with the demands of environmentalists to substitute oil, natural gas, coal (and, for other reasons, nuclear) energy sources with others that do not contribute to global warming and that do not pose immediate threats to communities and ecologies through pollution. It is important that the terms 'alternative energy' and 'sustainable' or 'renewable' energy are not conflated.

In recent years there have been moves in many countries to increase the contribution of wind power and hydropower to electricity generation. In Europe, Kyoto commitments have led Germany to say it will boost wind power's share of electricity generation to 15 per cent by 2030. Denmark has already reached 12 per cent and is targeting 50 per cent by 2030. In Britain, a consequence of government pledges to exceed Kyoto commitments has been a reopening of the debate over nuclear power, with some saying the promises can only be met by rowing against the European tide of nuclear phase-out.

Yet schemes to develop alternative energy sources are stimulated primarily by geopolitical and economic considerations. This is implicit in the IEA's observation, quoted above, that the oil price hikes of the 1970s had done more to slow demand growth and reduce energy use intensity than the policy pledges of the 1990s.

In early 1973 – months before the major price rises – President Nixon sent to Congress a series of proposals to conserve energy while boosting domestic production of oil, proposals aimed at reducing imports as the administration became concerned about the growing influence of OPEC. A year later, his response to the boycott and the price rises was Project Independence, a quest for self-sufficiency in energy by 1980 that echoed Eisenhower's massive support for domestic oil producers. It was in this context that the department of energy was asked to look at ways of developing the commercial application of non-oil and natural gas energy sources. In the next decade, after the Iranian revolution, President Carter's outgoing State of the Union address noted that solar energy funding had been quadrupled, a synthetic fuel corporation set up, new energy conservation measures put in place. But the successes claimed for such measures included a

2 million barrels a day cut in oil imports, an all-time high in domestic oil exploration drilling, and domestic coal production at a record level. Carter targeted an ambitious 20 per cent as the proportion of energy he wanted generated from sustainable sources by 2000, but energy production and consumption were tools, he said, 'to achieving our ultimate national goal of relying primarily on secure sources of energy'.[20]

Two decades on and the US discourse is essentially unchanged. A Republican Policy Committee summary of President George W. Bush's energy policy act says it 'intends to provide a comprehensive national energy policy that balances domestic energy production with conservation and efficiency efforts to enhance the security of the United States and decrease dependence on foreign sources of fuel'. Again, the major 'green' initiative of providing $1.8 billion for research and development of hydrogen fuel technology in no way suggested a challenge to the perceived right of US citizens to use as much cheap carbon-based energy as they wished. There were no provisions on climate change, no targets for use of renewables, and no uprating of vehicle fuel efficiency standards. Political opposition had earlier stymied an attempt to open up the Alaskan wilderness to drilling.

'Alternative' in the official US lexicon means alternative to imports from sources deemed unreliable. So, in energy policy there, exploring alternative fuels sits cheek by jowl with diversification of foreign oil and gas supplies. Some alternatives are environmentally benign, some less climate-changing than others, some potentially worse. Some are simply means of accessing existing fuels in different ways, such as coal tar sands processing, coal gasification or exploitation of natural gas hydrate. Others, like clean coal technology seek to reset the terms of competition between existing carbon fuels or, like gas-to-liquids technology, make use of stranded assets.

## Evaluating the 'alternatives'

Hydrogen-fuel-cell advocates describe an efficient and benign technology, and one that car manufacturers concede to be a likely future path of vehicle propulsion. A brief look at some of the alternatives to orthodox oil and natural gas production and consumption will demonstrate that many simply reproduce dependence on oil and natural gas and that substantial progress towards reducing that dependence, short of cutting energy demand, is a long way off.

The fossil fuels – oil, natural gas and coal – are related, all being carbon residues from decayed organic matter. (That said, there is a group of Russian scientists that questions this fundamental belief of the geological world.) They often occur together and the distinction between one and another is sometimes blurred – as in the case of sticky, viscous bitumen or natural gas liquids. The similarity of their chemical composition means they can often substitute for one another or even be transformed into each other. Some of the earliest cars were fuelled by ground coal, and in some parts of the world it is common for motor vehicles to be powered by liquefied propane gas (LPG). Elsewhere, compressed natural gas is being promoted as an environmentally better alternative to petrol or diesel.

This substitutability leads to competition between the fossil fuels. Some have characterised coal as the fuel of the eighteenth and nineteenth centuries, oil as the fuel of the twentieth century and natural gas a fuel for the current century, albeit perhaps as a bridge to a hydrogen economy. This is too simple a view, not least because cost and availability will always play a major role in determining who uses which fuel for which application.

Furthermore, changes to the fuel mix do not happen quickly: the IEA projects coal demand growing at 1.4 per cent to 2030, against 1.6 per cent for oil and 2.4 per cent for natural gas, but that still means that coal's share only slips from 26 per cent of the total to 24 per cent in three decades, with oil going from 38 per cent to 37 per cent. Natural gas accounts for a larger shift from 23 per cent to 28 per cent, largely at the expense of coal and nuclear power.[21] Some 60 per cent of new consumption of natural gas will be for power generation. Current, established technology makes natural-gas-powered generation, where available, cheaper, more efficient and less environmentally damaging than using coal or oil. Natural gas produces virtually no sulphur dioxide, less nitrogen oxides than oil or coal and its emissions of carbon dioxide are 40–50 per cent less than for coal and 25–30 per cent less than for oil.[22]

Yet coal can be cleaned up – at a price. There is a range of technology in production and development that can improve coal's efficiency, and so reduce the amount burnt and thus the emissions, as well as technology to reduce the emissions from that which is burnt. The World Coal Institute argues that, combined with measures to reabsorb or store carbon dioxide, coal can be a 'clean' fuel.

The question comes down to how much an economy is prepared to pay to be how much cleaner. In the US, where domestic sources will become increasingly expensive to produce as cheaper reserves deplete, natural gas loses its price advantage not only over imported liquefied natural gas but also to advanced clean coal technology, when prices are around $4 per million cubic feet.[23] For China, the forecast rate of changeover from coal to natural gas may be revised downwards as incremental volumes of gas delivered by pipeline or as LNG look increasingly expensive. According to the industry newspaper *Upstream*, natural gas could account for 12 per cent of the country's energy mix in 2010 if prices can be kept in the $3–4 per million British thermal units range, up from 3 per cent. But new supplies are costed at more than \$4, meaning the contribution of natural gas is now projected at 6 per cent by the end of the decade.[24]

Just as technological advance has made it commercially viable to access oil and natural gas from far under the seabed or from high-pressure and high-temperature reservoirs, so they can be extracted from non-conventional sources if the cost of production is competitive at prevailing world prices for conventionally won volumes. Interest is growing in gas hydrates, a frozen mixture of water, natural gas, mud and sand that occurs where conventional oil and natural gas do not – such as Japan, which is entirely dependent on imports. There are a number of ways in which the natural gas can be freed from the hydrate solid, and Japan envisages production in 2012–16. Potential reserves of natural gas in hydrates worldwide could exceed all reserves of all other fossil fuels.[25] But the theory is irrelevant unless the reserves do prove to be in the right place and accessible at costs consumers are willing to pay. Factored into those costs are whatever value they choose to put on control of supply – reduced import dependence – and environmental factors.

More established as alternative sources of natural gas and oil are coal-bed methane and oil sands production. Natural gas frequently occurs with coal, just as it does with oil. Indeed, its explosiveness poses a massive danger for mineworkers. Coal-bed methane is of a high quality and is relatively easy to exploit. It provides some 7 per cent of US gas production. The coal industry in Kansas is all but dead, but methane output is thriving. Elsewhere in North America, energy group Suncor is looking not only at producing coal-bed methane but also at forcing the gas out using carbon dioxide, which would replace it in the coal seams and so not be emitted into the atmosphere.[26] As North Sea reserves run down and the UK becomes a net importer of natural gas, interest has grown in sourcing gas from coal beds.

The IEA sees oil from non-conventional sources accounting for 8 per cent of world supply by 2030, some 9.9 million barrels a day, sharply up from 1.1 million barrels a day in 2000.[27] Most of this will come from oil sands in Canada and the heavy bituminous crude now being exploited in Venezuela. As with gas hydrates, the global reserve estimates are staggering for these heavy, viscous oils – three times known reserves of conventional oil. As with gas hydrates, this takes no account of location or cost.

The Canadian province of Alberta is the main oil-producing area, and some 40 per cent of its oil output in 2002 was from oil sands, equivalent to a third of national output and forecast to rise rapidly to 50 per cent. Some two tonnes of oil sands must be dug up to produce one barrel of oil. Of the 829,000 barrels a day produced in 2002, some 435,000 barrels a day were upgraded and used as fuel, and the rest sold as bitumen.[28] However, the scale of expansion of production in Alberta is not a given. Even with oil prices at decade highs, in early 2004 cost overruns were causing concerns over some projects.[29] Venezuelan non-conventional oil comes primarily from the Orinoco belt where over 300,000 barrels a day was produced in 2001, forecast to more than treble inside a decade. The oil produced is either upgraded or emulsified to produce a proprietary generation fuel called Orimulsion.

Another source of oil is natural gas. The basic technology for this conversion has been around since the 1920s, typically interesting governments without easy access to oil such as the apartheid regime in South Africa. Indeed, Sasol, the South African energy company, was and remains a leading proponent of the technology. From a tiny output today, gas–to–liquid technology is seen by the IEA as providing 2.3 million barrels a day by 2030. The main suppliers of natural gas for conversion will be gas–rich countries like Qatar and Iran that want to diversify away from piped natural gas and LNG exports. For both of these countries, the gas-to-liquids route meshes with broader ambitions to develop their downstream oil and petrochemical industries. As the two have unresolved claims over the Khuff gas formation, it also allows each of them to develop rapidly reserves they claim for themselves before the other can do so.

Proponents of the technology argue it allows for the commercialisation of gas reserves in the Middle East, Latin America, North and West Africa and Australasia that would otherwise be stranded without a market. They also point to the relative purity of the fuels produced – low in sulphur, nitrogen free, and with a high cetane count that pleases refiners. The Bintulu plant operated by Shell in Malaysia has been running as a pilot project since 1993. Two commercial-scale plants are planned in Qatar.

However, others argue the economics are uncertain. The technology has yet to be proven on a large scale and this will give financiers pause for thought when they match gas-to-liquids projects against others competing for their money. Then, while somewhere like Qatar might be able to provide gas to a plant at very low cost and the material coming out the other end might be of high quality, local demand is limited, meaning transport costs to OECD countries will be incurred.[30]

A number of renewable energy sources are seen as contributing to energy needed for power generation by countries reducing their fossil fuel dependence. These include wind power – already making a sizeable contribution in Denmark and Germany, for example – solar power and wave power. Hydro-power, electricity generated by water flow, has long been important in many countries – Norway being a prime example. But each has drawbacks. Solar generation on a large scale requires equally large-scale use of land for the panels currently developed, raising dubious neocolonial talk of using vast tracts of the Sahara to provide power for Europe. Because of difficulties in storing electricity, solar and wind power are regarded as too 'spotty' to rely on for more than a portion of power – no wind, no power; no sun, no power. To benefit from hydro-power you need water and mountains, and years of low rainfall reduce output. Hydro-power's contribution to the energy mix is expected to decline, in large part because of the contentiousness of both control of water and dam building in many developing regions. Wave power is relatively untested. (Nuclear power's contribution is already waning with phase-out taking place in Europe and the US. This said, its supporters argue it provides a way of meeting environmental targets.)

Near-term alternatives to petrol and diesel as transport fuels are similarly seen as parts of a patchwork. Cars can be run on almost any type of oil, including cooking oil. In parts of Europe and Latin America, bio-fuel from vegetation makes a contribution to overall fuel use. Liquefied propane gas has long been used, particularly in company car fleets. Compressed natural gas is being trialled in the UK, for example. Current thinking in much of the automotive industry and beyond is that hybrid vehicles are the way to reduce emissions in the next few years. These are vehicles that swap between use of battery power and liquid fuel according to circumstances.

## Hydrogen economy: another hydrocarbon economy?

One might imagine that the quest to transform the global economy from one based on hydrocarbons to one fuelled by hydrogen emerged in the late twentieth century, born of scientific advances, industrialised-country fears of dependence on former colonies, and growing realisation of the environmental catastrophes global warming will bring. In fact, the first combustion engine to be built in the early years of the nineteenth century was fuelled by hydrogen; the fuel cell was invented before the middle of the nineteenth century, and Jules Verne, the doyen of science-fiction writing, conjured up a story in 1875 in which water took the place of coal as a fuel.

The time needed for scientific breakthroughs and inventions to gain acceptance and widespread use has been studied. One theory has it that it takes around fifty years for new technologies to gain currency. By that measure, the hydrogen economy should be upon us. Leaving aside the early work and musings of the nineteenth century, in the 1950s the US Air Force was testing hydrogen as a fuel for aircraft. Some companies, such as FuelCell Energy in the US, have been developing and producing hydrogen-powered generators for several decades. The automotive industry is working on assumptions that hydrogen will not begin to be a significant motor fuel until around 2015. The IEA believes it will be thirty years before hydrogen becomes more than a minor part of the energy mix, unless there is a significant change in governmental policy and technological progress.

So why is there so little evidence of a shift towards hydrogen? It is not just a matter of resistance by oil companies or others with a vested interest in maintaining the hydrocarbon economy. Indeed, they stand to profit from a shift to hydrogen. The oil companies are driven by their shareholders' quest for profit not by attachment to oil and gas. In the past they have hedged their position by buying up coal mines, and they already have important investments in renewable energy research, development and deployment. And, for now, a shift towards hydrogen actually offers a new market for the fossil fuels.

The economic and environmental cases for a switch to hydrogen have yet to be made. When hydrogen is used as a fuel it gives off next to no emissions apart from water, seemingly the solution to our mounting problem of greenhouse gas emissions and global warming. And hydrogen is available in inexhaustible quantities from water. But therein lies both a major problem and another reason why development of hydrogen fuel cells is not an immediate threat to the oil and gas industries. Hydrogen in itself is not an energy source but, like electricity, a carrier of energy derived elsewhere. Hydrogen, like electricity is not available without being produced. Currently there are two ways of doing this: the one that accounts for 98 per cent of current hydrogen production (largely for the fertiliser and industrial gases industries) is by chemically splitting it from hydrocarbons; the other is by electrolysis.

So, the prospect of massive new demand for hydrogen also opens up the prospect of a new market for oil and gas producers as suppliers of feedstock to hydrogen plants, just as they currently supply feedstock to conventional power stations. The coal industry is positioning itself as provider of fuel to produce hydrogen, an irony given coal's image as the dirty fuel. For the governments of the US, Japan and other high-energy-consuming developed economies with coal reserves, hydrogen fuel cells running on hydrogen produced from domestic coal would also reduce dependence on imported energy. As a report by finance house Merrill Lynch's new energy technology investment manager noted, 'the US government's vocal support of fuel cell vehicles is not primarily aimed at reducing emissions but to reduce dependence on foreign oil'.[31] There has even been the suggestion that the funding for hydrogen cell research announced by George W. Bush was 'an effort to deflect a more politically painful, but immediately plausible policy to make a here and now effort to switch to hybrid automotive technologies that could immediately reduce consumption through increased efficiency'.[32]

Production of hydrogen by electrolysis requires electricity, and, of course, unless that was generated by non-emitting sources, such as solar or wind power (or nuclear), that too would require use of coal, gas or oil.

Hydrogen fuel cells are more efficient than most other forms of power generation (although combined cycle gas plants certainly run them close), so a move towards on-site generation for the commercial sector would bring some reduction in greenhouse gas emissions. But a recent research note by the secretariat of the IEA was underwhelmed, saying that the changeover in prospect for the coming years would not significantly affect the fuel mix because most fuel cells would rely on gas and the greater efficiency of the cells would just 'slightly decarbonise the power generation'.[33]

That same document is worth quoting at some length on the scale of the economic and environmental problems that will exist until a new and commercially viable hydrogen production technology is developed and accepted or current technology made massively more efficient:

> to date apart from reforming and electrolysis no alternative route has been demonstrated and neither approach is competitive on the energy market. For electrolysis, this is partly a function of the efficiency, which is low. A simple example illustrates the point: replacing all the transportation fuel used in France with hydrogen would require around four times the present electricity consumption (i.e. around 700 Twh [terawatt hours] additional consumption). Producing this electricity would require the building of 60 new nuclear plants of 1,500 MW [Megawatts], or covering 6 per cent of French territory with approximately 350,000 wind turbines or covering 1 per cent of the land with PV [photovoltaic] cells (at an even higher cost). High costs also apply to the currently available technologies of $CO_2$ capture and storage. If the 700 Twh are provided by natural gas (the least costly fuel from which to extract $CO_2$), capture costs alone would lead to approximately a doubling in the operating costs – without the costs of transport or storage. While these technologies are currently available – and even in commercial use – the scale of these operations is several orders of magnitude lower than required for commercial energy application at a national level.[34]

Once the problems of hydrogen production are addressed, there are more concerning its storage and distribution.

The immensity of the environmental challenge is evident just by reminding ourselves of projections for energy demand growth. In 2000, world commercial primary energy demand – that is, excluding the 1.6 billion dependent on biomass in the developing world – was some 9.2 billion tonnes of oil equivalent. It will have increased to some 15.3 billion by 2030. Oil, gas and coal accounted for around 85 per cent of the 2000 total and will account for at least as much in 2030, according to the IEA's reference case. Under its Alternative Policy Scenario, which assumes policy changes under consideration are implemented, demand would be scarcely lower than in the reference case in 2010 but 9 per cent lower than the reference case scenario in 2030. Slightly more encouragingly, under the alternative scenario, OECD emissions would peak after 2020 and the slowdown in their growth would be somewhat higher than that for energy demand.[35]

# CONCLUSION

## Posing the questions

There is no doubt that oil and natural gas consumption will continue to rise, and rise strongly, in coming years. There may be variance in the growth rates and time horizons used by different international bodies, governments and companies but the trends are undisputed. Looking as far out as 2025 or 2030, oil remains the dominant energy source, although the role of natural gas will continue to grow. The hydrogen economy has been envisaged since the nineteenth century but for now the most direct route to it lies through fossil fuels. Kyle McSlarrow, US deputy secretary for energy, said candidly: 'What we're trying to do with the hydrogen economy is to take a lot of domestic resources, that is coal, natural gas, nuclear and so forth, and use them for the production of hydrogen.'[1]

The proportion of demand accounted for by developing countries is increasing strongly. In 2001 developing countries consumed 64 per cent as much oil as industrialised countries. By 2025, they will consume 94 per cent as much, according to US government projections.[2] Total demand in Asian developing economies will double in the time frame. By 2030 non–OECD countries' share of oil demand will have reached 50 per cent from 38 per cent now.[3] Natural gas demand will grow most rapidly in the developing world, but lack of infrastructure there means that OECD countries and those in eastern Europe and the former Soviet Union will continue to account for the bulk of consumption.

A corollary of this is that global carbon dioxide emissions will continue to climb − by over 50 per cent in the period to 2025 according to the US figures. Developing countries will account for some 60 per cent of the rise, those projections show. The IEA calculates that in 2000 the breakdown of emissions among OECD, developing and transition economies was 55 per cent, 34 per cent, 11 per cent, respectively. By 2030 that is seen as changing to 43 per cent, 47 per cent, 10 per cent.

The reasons for this are plain. Not only are major developing countries building industries to satisfy domestic demand but they are increasingly acting as the factories for the industrialised − ever more post-industrial − countries. Without developed natural gas infrastructure, without the financial resources to abate carbon emissions, and with heavier reliance on coal, the emissions of export industries are higher than they would be if Western corporations had not migrated their production in search of lower labour costs (and often laxer environmental controls). Oil-importing developing countries use twice as much oil to produce one unit of economic output as do developed countries.[4] At the same time, urbanisation and improving transport infrastructure are giving access to oil-based energy to communities hitherto reliant on biomass sources.

While the demand and emission projections for the developing world are high, per capita consumption and per capita emissions are and will remain way below those of the energy-guzzling OECD nations, however. So, for example, developing countries, have a per capita electricity consumption of around a seventh of that in the OECD, and by 2030 this is expected to have narrowed only to around a fifth or a sixth. Per capita emissions in the developing world will rise to 4.5 tonnes in China, 1.6 tonnes in India, 1.3 tonnes in sub-Saharan Africa by 2030, but in the OECD they are already approaching 12 tonnes and will rise to around 13 tonnes.[5]

The continued dominance of hydrocarbons in the global energy mix means continuation of the economic and hence political role of oil and gas for producer and consumer countries alike. The volatility of oil prices (with a knock-on effect on natural gas prices) will remain a key determinant of the revenues available to producer-country governments. The dominance will also continue to impact – to a disputed extent – on the economies of the industrialised countries and, to a larger extent, on those of developing countries. One way of looking at this is through economists' models of the impact of oil price rises. In 2000 the IMF modelled the effects of a sustained $5 a barrel rise, and three years later the IEA considered a $10 a barrel rise. The exact figures projected should not be taken too literally but the overall conclusions are apposite given that the average price for the OPEC basket of crudes did rise from $23.12 a barrel in 2001 to $28.16 in 2003 and $30.75 in the first quarter of 2004, rising to over $45 in October 2004.

The IMF paper[6] shows that a five-year $5 rise in oil prices would boost the current account surplus of the United Arab Emirates by more than 5 per cent of GDP. Russia would be another major gainer, but for some oil producers such as Mexico and Malaysia the overall consequences would be negative due to the effects on other trade with consumer countries. For the group of OPEC countries, the net trade balance would improve by 6.5 per cent of GDP, even allowing for secondary effects. As much as 75 per cent of the extra revenues would be spent on imports after three years if precedent were followed. Although the report notes a determination to avoid boom–bust cycles of previous windfalls, so high an estimate for imports suggests continued recycling of oil earnings back into the pockets of OECD corporations and governments.

Saudi fears of growing budget deficit have been eased by oil prices remaining high, and the kingdom had a revised projected surplus of $5.3 billion for 2004.[7] For the countries of the Gulf Cooperation Council, growth in oil revenues was seen powering a 5 per cent rise in GDP in 2004 and expansionary fiscal policies.[8] But the revenue roller-coaster impact of price volatility on oil-export-dependent countries remains. OPEC oil export revenues rose 24 per cent in 2003 to $242 billion with a 5 per cent fall expected to follow.[9] For Saudi Arabia the drop in 2004 was seen at 14 per cent but was delayed by further price rises that year. The World Bank estimates that of Russia's 7.2 per cent economic growth in 2003, some 3 per cent was attributable to rising oil prices. Russian growth has only exceeded 5 per cent in recent years when oil prices were rising. The lesson the World Bank draws is that for Russia to achieve its objective of doubling GDP in ten years either oil prices must continue to rise or major structural reform must take place.[10]

As experience has taught exporter countries, of course, high oil prices are not an unalloyed blessing. As Saudi Arabia has argued over decades, to push prices so high as to cramp demand is to starve the goose that lays the golden eggs.

The vulnerability of OECD countries to sharp rises in the oil price is much less now than it was in the past, due for the most part to lower energy intensity. In the early 1970s, energy expenditure accounted for 8 per cent of US GDP, 5 per cent of that being oil and 1 per cent natural gas. By 1981 that had risen to 14 per cent, 8 per cent and 2 per cent, respectively. By 2001, the figures were down at 7 per cent, 3.5 per cent and 1 per cent, respectively.[11] Nonetheless, after the run up in prices at the end of the 1990s, results statements of countless companies looked incomplete without a couple of lines referring to the negative effects of higher energy costs. As prices, particularly indicative futures prices, of oil and natural gas increased further in 2004, market watchers increasingly looked for guidance to the likes of Alan Greenspan, veteran chairman of the US Federal Reserve. As it happened, when the US unveiled a higher than expected fiscal deficit in May 2004, oil price rises only accounted for around 13 per cent of the overshoot, a far higher percentage being attributed to the costs of civil aircraft. Also, the IEA's market report of the same month showed an unexpected surge in demand for oil from OECD countries.

The 1973–74 rise in oil prices caused a direct trade loss to the OECD countries of some 2.5 per cent of GDP, according to the IMF. Others suggest that the contribution of oil prices to the estimated $350 billion loss of output during the following recession was even higher. The terms-of-trade impact on the OECD countries of the 1979–80 oil shock was even greater at 3.5 per cent of GDP, the same IMF report says, but the consumer countries had policies in place this time round and held down wages to contain the inflationary effect. The more minor and short-lived increase around the 1990 Gulf crisis had little effect.

The IMF paper postulating a $5 a barrel rise in prices, sustained for five years, suggests that industrialised country GDP would be 0.3 per cent lower than otherwise for a couple of years before recovering. Their trade balance would suffer reductions of some $20–27 billion a year. The IEA notes studies that estimate a sustained increase of $10 a barrel would cut GDP growth by 0.6 per cent in the industrialised countries. Modelling a shorter run $10 a barrel rise, the agency sees the US GDP growth just 0.15 per cent lower, and 0.2 per cent and 0.3 per cent for the euro zone and Japan, respectively. Elsewhere, the IEA argues, world GDP growth might have been half a percentage point higher annually in 2002–04 if oil prices had remained at mid-2001 levels.[12]

Notwithstanding some expressions of concern over oil prices in the futures markets, however, US economic growth was accelerating as 2004 progressed, even if Europe and Japan lagged, causing the IEA to suggest that oil prices were exacerbating unemployment and budget deficit problems.

It is developing oil-importing countries that bear the brunt of higher prices. Their energy intensity is greater and their demand is growing, often faster than their ability to pay. Also, many of them subsidise some fuel prices. Very poor, highly indebted countries are the worst affected. The volatility of the cost of so important an import item also renders planning difficult. For Mali, a $5 rise increases the current account deficit by 1.25 per cent of GDP, for Belarus 1.6 per cent. Of the larger developing country economies, worst affected are India, South Korea, Pakistan, the Philippines, Thailand and Turkey. India's GDP suffers by 0.5 per cent and South Korea's by 0.9 per cent, for example. For China the shock amounts to 0.4 per cent of GDP. Under the IEA's $10 rise scenario, developing countries' average GDP growth slows by 0.75 per cent.

On the face it, what a price rise does is simply transfer money from the pockets of importing countries to those of exporting countries. Economists hold that it is more complicated than that and there is a reduction of global economic growth. One reason, they argue, is that those losing income – importers – tend to reduce their spending in response by more than those gaining income – exporters – increase theirs, creating a net fall in demand. Also, the increase in oil prices does feed through into oil-exporting-country economies both directly and through increased costs of manufactured imports. On top of that, there are wider inflationary effects and impacts on financial markets.

Nonetheless, this economistic argument against higher prices deserves political scrutiny for it suggests there is a global good in a higher global growth rate. In an international economy where the powerful players of North America and Europe preach free trade while carefully maintaining their own subsidy schemes and using their weight in the World Trade Organisation to bolster their dominance, this suggestion is highly questionable. UN Conference on Trade and Development data show the share of developing countries in the global export of all fuels to be much higher at 57.8 per cent (with eastern Europe accounting for another 10.1 per cent) than for ores or agricultural raw materials or food items.

Ever since oil and, later, natural gas became strategic commodities, the imperial and then post-imperial powers have sought to maintain control, direct or indirect, over the supply and pricing of hydrocarbons. During the era of concessions and posted prices this was blatant. Since OPEC wrested production decisions from the hands of the companies and their governments it has been treated as a bogeyman, an unacceptable cartel, when prices threaten the profit levels of energy-consuming corporations based in the industrialised countries. Similarly, it has been blamed for higher costs for consumer-country motorists even though the tax take from pump prices outside of the US exceeds the cost of the crude oil refined to make the fuel. Yet in times of political crisis OPEC has been relied on to ensure supplies of oil and to control the price at which it is supplied. Further, OPEC's defence of prices both bolsters the profits of major oil companies and keeps smaller companies' heads above water.

Is there not an argument that justice and equity are better served by a lower global economic growth rate in which a greater proportion of wealth accrues to oil-exporting developing countries? After all, between 1996 and 2000 the Group of Seven – members including the richest and most powerful countries in the world – garnered taxes on oil worth $1,300 billion while the oil revenue accruing to OPEC members was $850 billion.[13] That simple but telling fact leaves aside a slew of other arguments why wealthy oil- and natural-gas-importing countries should pay more to developing producer countries, among these that reserves are irreplaceable and so warrant a premium, that real prices have been in long-term decline, and that hydrocarbons should be priced against alternative energy sources to find their true worth.

One problem here, of course, is that, as the economists' models demonstrate, higher prices are likely to hurt oil-importing developing economies more than wealthy industrialised countries. There is an argument for nudging the likes of India and Brazil and China and Turkey in the direction of greater energy efficiency. Sugar cane producers such as Brazil and India could almost eliminate the need for fossil fuels for transport by converting to biofuel, using cane as feedstock and reducing carbon dioxide emissions considerably. On the other hand, a corollary might well be greater use of coal for power generation.

Some argue that developing countries have an opportunity to skip some of the more severely environmentally damaging technologies that powered the development of the industrialised world. Others see this argument as a veiled move to force the developing world to accept slower economic development to mitigate the environmental damage done by the industrialised world. In the absence of mitigating measures it is harder to sustain the argument for higher oil and natural gas prices as a tool for change when considering Moldova or Guyana or Benin.

The other problem with the argument for higher oil and natural gas prices as a means of redistributing wealth is one that has been laboured in this book: the very social and political conditions that dependency on hydrocarbon exports entrenches. Equity, justice, redistributive principles, let alone anything more politically radical, are not served by channelling vast rents into the coffers of self-enriching elites, be they royalties of dubious provenance, military dictatorships, or politicians in league with home-grown or foreign corporate interests. Dependence on hydrocarbon exports in developing and transitional economies is associated with de-development, worsening poverty and immiseration, civil conflict and authoritarian rule. The tendency of oil and gas rents to promote challenges to the unity of existing states is a constant threat to central governments. One year into the occupation of Iraq and there were already calls from the south of the country for control over revenues and the creation of a federal state. If those calls are not answered, will more insistent and radical demands follow? Amid the worsening violence in Nigeria's Delta region, the siphoning of oil from pipelines by militias is increasingly explained in quasi-political populist terms, banditry mixed with rejection of government from Abuja.

Exporting countries have been singularly unsuccessful in diversifying away from oil and natural gas, 'sowing the oil'. In part this is because the competition for rent has soaked up political and economic energy. In part it is because moving downstream into refining and petrochemicals has merely enlarged the boundaries of an enclave industry. In the past, diversification plans have led to inappropriate projects and the proliferation of white elephants.

In recent years there have been moves by non-governmental organisations and UN bodies to force transparency into project development plans. The Publish What You Pay campaign urges extractive industry companies to reveal sums spent securing exploration and production licences. In 1999, UN secretary-general Kofi Annan launched the notion of a Global Compact between major corporations and UN agencies. The companies would adhere to nine key principles in the areas of human and labour rights and environmental good practice. The Chad–Cameroon oil production and pipeline project has established a new model of control and supervision of rents under World Bank tutelage.

What can such initiatives achieve? The campaign to achieve transparency in the securing by companies of licences is positive inasmuch as it helps to prevent or expose corruption and mis-directing of revenue. To that extent it might encourage financial institutions to scrutinise operations in a given country more closely. Indeed, there is evidence of closer inspection of projects. However, corruption in the sense of illegal self-enrichment is only a minor manifestation of the allocation of oil rent. As pointed out earlier, the core problem is one of economic structure and political power. The governments that oversee the partisan distribu-tion of oil wealth are recognised and legitimate governments. The circumscribed diagnostic of Angola's oil revenues commissioned by the World Bank found that $4 billion had strayed between 1997 and 2002, yet in 2004 the government was still able to obtain a concessional loan of $2 billion from China and the state oil company went to Standard Chartered Bank to put together another of the much-criticised oil-backed loans, this one worth $2.5 billion. Meanwhile, to the north, despite all the criticisms of the system, the award of licences for the Nigeria and São Tomé joint development zone was to be made largely (though not exclusively) on the basis of signature bonuses.

For good or bad, the controls over revenues from the Chad–Cameroon project are limited in duration. And the spirit in which they were to be treated was demonstrated when in 1998 Chadian president Idris Deby promptly spent $4 million of the initial payout to the government of $25 million on arms purchases.

Global Compact has attracted big-name companies but the reputations of those companies quickly sullied the reputation of the initiative. Among the early joiners were demons of lobbyists for the very human, labour and environmental rights the compact was supposed to promote. Alongside Shell and BP were the likes of Nike, Rio Tinto and Novartis, with reputations for sweatshop labour, environmental degradation, and aggressive promotion of genetically engineered agriculture. Global Compact's voluntary status simply distracts attention from avoidance of statutory obligations, critics say. At the same time many trade unionists would say it was a very good advance when the international confederation of energy workers' unions, ICEM, persuaded the large Russian oil company Lukoil to sign an agreement based on the compact. But in mid-2004, Fred Higgs, the ICEM secretary-general issued a strongly worded report saying that if the compact was not given the powers to expel companies that had signed up but not performed then trade-union involvement in the body would be jeopardised.[14]

If little appears to have changed or to be changing in the social and political composition of established exporting countries, perhaps more depressing are the signs of replication of the conditions for conflict, poverty and inequality in countries that are, or may become, exporters. Tiny and impoverished São Tomé e Príncipe was set to gain some $200 million in 2004 from its share of oil company payments to explore in the Nigeria–São Tomé joint development zone. The sum represents 50 times average annual export earnings. As one report noted:

> Although it will be years before oil is actually produced, the prospect of new wealth has already heightened instability in the island state where there have been frequent changes of government and concerns about corruption.
> The issue surfaced in July [2003] when Mr de Menezes [the president] was briefly unseated by a military coup. He was restored as a result of international pressure and signed a deal with the rebels who demanded a greater say in how the country's earnings from crude oil are spent.

> There were also concerns about the transparency of the [licence] auction process.[15]

An industry newspaper reported that São Tomé 'will soon have to follow its big neighbour Nigeria in having to manage internal dissent over upstream oil privileges'. It continued:

> São Tomé is facing fresh opposition from minority communities claiming prior rights to the expected offshore bonanza.
>
> While the bulk of the state's 135,000 population live on São Tomé, only about 5,000 live on Príncipe, which, as the more northerly of the two can claim a closer proximity to the eight prized oil blocks bid under the ongoing licensing round....
>
> The island's sole national assemblyman, Simao Lavares, even called for independence.... Few believe the island's remonstrations represent more than opening salvoes in a looming battle for future oil revenue allocations development funding.[16]

Equatorial Guinea is a new oil producer already exporting at a rate of several hundred thousand barrels a day and is the prospective location for a major LNG plant exporting to Europe and North America. *Global Witness*[17] notes a GDP growth rate of a phenomenal 60 per cent in 2001 as oil earnings kicked in. Revenues from oil were set to triple between 2001 and 2003, yet UN agencies, the World Bank, the IMF and the US government variously noted no improvement in the economic and social conditions of the population, most of whom live in extreme poverty; strong evidence of misappropriation of oil revenues by the elite; and declining social indicators.

The president, Teodoro Obiang, who came to power through a coup against his uncle, rules through a tight-knit clique that employs brutality and repression of dissent as a matter of course. Production-sharing agreements with oil companies may well have been ineptly negotiated, the government take being very low, but with perhaps $500 million unaccounted for and little in the way of formal accounting for oil revenues, this may be of little concern to the regime. In March 2004 there was an unsuccessful but not unexpected coup attempt against President Obiang.

In the Maghreb, the first oil development offshore Mauritania will net the government $100 million a year after capital cost recovery by the companies. This will increase government revenues by around 50 per cent. A second development will follow and there is early talk of the country becoming an LNG exporter. But Mauritania fits well into the profile of countries whose populace is likely to experience not a boom but a worsening of economic conditions as the hydrocarbon sector takes off.

Coups d'état have been the motor of change in Mauritania since the country became independent. Its society has tribal cleavages. There are periodic clashes between settled agriculturalists and the pastoralists in the south. Relations with Morocco and Senegal are uncomfortable and the country is a peripheral player in the Western Sahara conflict. Additionally, its domestic politics have been a playground for interests ranging from the Iraqi Baath Party to the Israeli state. There was a coup attempt in mid-2003, just as the oil companies were firming up plans to develop the Chinguetti field, and further reports of attempted seizures of power the following year as the companies firmed up further prospects.

If the exploitation of hydrocarbons poses political questions about the distribution and employment of revenues within producer countries, it does so within an international context. Oil and natural gas are inseparable from geopolitics. Since the imperial powers committed to the transition from coal to oil they have sought to ensure its supply through power relationships that have varied from the outright plunder enshrined in the concessions system to the exertion of influence over client states, the undermining of non-compliant regimes, the garrisoning of producer regions, and the extension of political and economic influence over new producer countries. Western-dominated international financial institutions have been used to encourage liberalisation but in Iraq the occupation forces have simply imposed their own corporations on large parts of the energy sector with the aim of securing technical and financial control, creating a fait accompli that a national government will find hard to reverse. Meanwhile, the whereabouts of tens of billions of dollars of Iraqi oil earnings was being investigated by no fewer than ten separate enquiries one year after the invasion. The probes were examining not just the alleged corruption of the oil-for-food programme that existed during much of the time Iraq was under UN sanctions but also the lack of accountability of the occupation regime's spending of $20 billion of oil earnings. The occupation flew the banner of fiscal transparency and then proceeded to trample it into the dirt, demonstrating once more the pernicious influence of rent in a country with unaccountable government.

Relations with producers have been and continue to be determined by the usefulness of incumbent regimes in bolstering post-colonial control over hydrocarbon reserves. The totalitarian Iran of the shah was a key ally when Arab nationalism was perceived as a threat to OECD interests. Saddam Hussein was armed throughout his war with post-revolutionary Iran, only demonised after his invasion of Kuwait in 1990. The intolerance and autocracy of the conservative Saudi Arabian ruling clique was glossed over for decades as long as it ensured OPEC did not pursue the strategies of its price hawks. Then, as the suspicion grew in Washington that the clique was losing its grip on Saudi society, neo-conservative background music increased in volume, harping on the theme that US interests would be better secured by an Iraq controlled directly or indirectly from the White House.

In North Africa, Libya is fawned upon because it has agreed not only to encourage the oil companies to come back in but has also abandoned its role as agent provocateur in the Middle

East and Africa. Algeria is now a favourite of the White House after suppressing its Islamic rebellion and welcoming in the oil companies.

In Africa there have been and will be no scruples in dealing with regimes, however distasteful. French oil company and state organ Elf set the standard, not only enriching established dictators but cheerfully dealing with both sides in conflicts. For all the bleating from the Blair government in the UK about transparency in commercial operations, there is not and never has been any question of oil companies refusing to operate in Nigeria or Angola. As new opportunities arise in countries such as Equatorial Guinea or São Tomé, the talk is not of regime change but of strengthening military links to further secure commercial ties.

In Central Asia, the social and political inequalities of Kazakhstan and Turkmenistan are overlooked as long as the regimes ensure the oil and natural gas flows in the right direction. By contrast, in Latin America, the eccentricities of Hugo Chavez have attracted less favourable attention from the US as his populist nationalist rhetoric has threatened privatisation programmes in the oil industry and, directly contrary to his predecessor, encouraged more robust policies by OPEC.

The newly independent state of East Timor, which was established after decades of occupation, the brutality of which verged on the genocidal, is one of the poorest in the world. Australia was happy to deal with the Indonesian occupier of East Timor in order to secure a share of the offshore oil and natural gas of the Timor Gap. Since independence the Australian government has turned the screws on the government in Dili. In 2002 it withdrew from the International Court of Justice process on maritime boundaries in an attempt to preserve boundaries agreed in 1972 with Jakarta that put large reserves inside Australian territorial water. Then it refused to commit to a time frame for determining boundaries with East Timor while pressuring it to agree a deal over the Sunrise natural gas fields that would give Dili only 18 per cent of revenues. The Timorese government said in 2004 that Canberra's greedy obstinacy was costing a country with a government budget measured in tens of millions of dollars some $350 million a year.[18]

As the fuel import requirements of China and India have increased, they have moved to secure production elsewhere. This has involved seeking entrées into countries and projects not already sewn up by incumbent players – that is, OECD oil companies and state corporations. That has led them to exploit political circumstances. Thus, for example, China's success in obtaining a role in the development of Saudi Arabian natural gas reserves may have resulted from the straining of relations between Riyadh and Washington. The new players have shown themselves no less willing than the OECD countries when it comes to dealing with unsavoury regimes – China, India and Malaysia all being keen participants in Sudan.

The environmental impact of fossil fuel use on the climate is proven. Climate change will impact on the global environment, indeed is already doing so in the view not only of environmental campaigners but also of the insurance industry. The effects will include crop migration, sea-level rise and changes in the distribution of diseases. These phenomena have profound political and humanitarian implications, most directly for poorer nations and social strata. Both the Netherlands and Bangladesh are threatened by sea-level rise but there is no comparison between the financial resources they can marshall to mitigate it.

Nowithstanding the belated ratification of the Kyoto Protocol by Russia's President Putin, in return for trade concessions from the EU, the response to global warming by the governments that matter has been entirely inadequate at the policy level, let alone that of implementation. Long before Kyoto it was too late to prevent global warming, but the laggardly approach of the powerful governments has ensured year-by-year, month-by-month, that the effects will be greater than if early, firm action had been taken and that it will take even longer to turn the tide.

Changing the energy mix can change the extent and rate at which greenhouse gases are generated. Natural gas is less bad than oil, and oil is less bad than dirty coal. Clean coal is substantially better than dirty coal. Maximising the use of biomass for vehicle fuel, running cars on liquid propane gas, accelerating the introduction of hybrid engines, expanding use of wind and solar and tidal power – all these are worth doing, but they only slow the juggernaut set rolling by the Industrial Revolution, they cannot stop it. The hydrogen economy is not just around the corner and, as we have seen, for the moment it does not hold out the prospect of replacement of fossil fuels but rather their redeployment, and possibly a redeployment that would strengthen the hand of consumer countries by diversifying their potential sources of primary fuel through greater use of coal.

There are two ways in which incremental additions to greenhouse gas emissions brought about by booming global energy demand could be cut back significantly and rapidly. The first is through the compulsory and widespread introduction of abatement technology. In dollars, euros and pounds the bill would be astronomical but in terms of economic growth forgone by the OECD economies, projections suggest it would be of the scale of a serious recession. The choice is there, the question is one of political will.

The second means of reducing greenhouse gas emissions is by reducing demand for fossil fuels through significant and sustained price increase. Only externally induced, major price shocks have succeeded in increasing energy efficiency, cutting intensity of use and reducing demand in the OECD countries. Governments with perspectives no longer than the electoral cycle find the challenge of fulfilling commitments to raise progressively vehicle fuel duty or climate-change levies challenging enough. There is next to no hope of them supporting rises of several tens of dollars a barrel (even if they stood to cream off much of the increase in the form of taxes). What is more likely, as the adventurism in the Middle East in 2003 showed, is that political and military incompetence in furtherance of strategic control of resources will endanger supply streams while prices are further boosted by the fears, scenarios, rumours and headlines that drive the virtual world of speculative trading.

Yet it is worth pointing out once more that if the rich consumer countries of the world have at least the notional options of massive adoption of abatement technology and policy change in response to an upward real price trend, those options are not there for many developing countries. Without the major developing countries adopting emissions reduction measures soon, action in the industrialised world is merely shutting the door after the horse has bolted. Again, the question is how developing countries would pay for abatement or massive increases in energy efficiency. Should the cost be met by the countries that have achieved their wealth through pollution and plunder of other countries' natural resources?

Even a cursory examination of the oil and natural gas sector brings us back time and again to profoundly political issues. The reality of life in many producer countries is one of instability at the economic and social levels, far from the 1970s myth of oil-rich sheikhdoms where a populace wealthy beyond the dreams of avarice basks in sun and sloth. The distribution of hydrocarbon rents poses uncomfortable questions about the distribution of political power and almost guarantees resentment and unrest among those outside of the charmed circles of patronage. Dissatisfaction over rent distribution, given the association between state and hydrocarbons, soon poses questions about the legitimacy of the state and the social relations it underpins. In countries where state building is a relatively new project, that questioning fans fears that do not exist in Norway or Canada. The enclave nature of the sector means there is relatively little evidence so far to suggest that oil and natural gas exports promote class confrontation.

At the global level, oil and natural gas are inseparable from geostrategy. The quest of the powerful consumer nations for access to energy on their own terms runs parallel to the clashes over agricultural subsidies or steel subsidies that bedevil world trade talks – subsidies for EU farmers or US cotton growers are imposed on the rest of the world even as the poorest countries are forced to liberalise in the name of free trade. Exporting cheap steel to the US is damned as dumping in Washington with trade sanctions imposed. Strains of rice developed by Indian farmers are patented by multinational agro corporations. In the energy sector, the natives of producer countries are good natives as long as they guarantee supply of oil and natural gas at prices that are low enough to be acceptable to companies and governments in the rich consumer countries and high enough to keep the nodding-donkey producers of Pennsylvania and the shareholders of the oil majors happy.

Yet when control of supply is perceived to be jeopardised, whether by the governments of producer countries, political forces within producer regions, or competition from strategic rivals, the armoury brought to bear is awesome: ranging from the tongue lashings from the IEA that OPEC attracts, to the replacement of Russian imperialism with US clientelism in Central Asia, to grand strategies for structural and political change in the Middle East and North Africa, to support for coup attempts in Latin

America. As the optics through which consumer-country energy 'security' is viewed in the powerful consumer countries have changed over the decades, something that has remained constant is the instability and insecurity their strategies have engendered. Russian concerns over the US dominance of Central Asia are intensifying. The potential for serious clashes of interests between China and the US over third-party energy supplies is growing. From the Caucasus through the Persian Gulf and across the Sahel to West Africa, the 'arc of instability' that corresponds with an arc of oil and natural gas reserves and transit routes has become a justification for interventionism that is guaranteed to exacerbate tension and promote conflict.

# Notes

## Chapter 1

1. 'Top World Oil Tables', www.eia.doe.gov.
2. Derived from *Annual Statistical Bulletin* of the Organisation of Petroleum Exporting Countries (OPEC), Vienna, 1997 and 2002.
3. *World Energy Outlook 2002*, International Energy Agency, Brussels, p. 90.
4. *Annual Energy Outlook 2003*, Energy Information Administration, Washington DC, p. 3.
5. Derived from *World Energy Outlook 2002*, p. 410.
6. Fiona Venn, *Oil Diplomacy in the Twentieth Century*, Macmillan, London, 1986, p. 139.
7. Extrapolated from *Annual Energy Outlook 2003*, p. 83.
8. *World Energy Outlook 2002*, p. 108.
9. Ibid., p. 117.
10. 'Top World Oil Tables'.
11. *Financial Times*, 11 September 2003.
12. 'Top World Oil Tables'.
13. BP Statistical Review, www.bp.com.
14. BG presentation to analysts, London, 13 November 2003.
15. 'Oil Field Mega Projects 2004', *Petroleum Review*, Energy Institute, January 2004.
16. That said, although the medium-term forecasts for investment in deep-water projects remained robust, in late 2003 oilfield service

companies complained that lacklustre financial performance was due in part to delays in the sanctioning of such projects by the oil companies.

17. *Petroleum Review*, Energy Institute, January 2004, p. 6.
18. All percentages derived from OPEC, *Annual Statistical Bulletin*, 1997 and 2002.
19. *World Energy Outlook 2002*, pp. 94–100.
20. Bright E. Okogu, *The Middle East and North Africa in a Changing Oil Market*, IMF, Washington DC, 2003, p. 7.
21. Eugene Khartukov and Ellen Starostina, 'Post-Soviet Oil Exports: Are the Russians Really Coming?', *OPEC Bulletin*, September–October 2003.
22. *World Energy Investment Outlook 2003*, International Energy Agency, Brussels, 2003.
23. BP trading statement to London Stock Exchange, 29 March 2004.
24. Company regulatory filings.
25. *World Energy Investment Outlook 2003*, p. 159.
26. Ibid., p. 205.
27. *Monthly Oil Market Report, July 2004*, IEA, Paris, July 2004.

## Chapter 2

1. Dow Jones Newswires, 1 March 2004
2. Energy Information Administration (EIA), *Major Non-Opec Countries Oil Revenues*, Washington DC, June 2003.
3. Goohoon Kwon, *Budgetary Impact of Oil Prices in Russia*, IMF, Washington DC, 2003.
4. Organisation of Petroleum Exporting Countries (OPEC), *Annual Statistical Bulletin 2002*, Vienna, 2002.
5. EIA, *Major Non-Opec Countries Oil Revenues*.
6. Energy Information Administration, *Opec Revenues Fact Sheet*, June 2003.
7. International Crisis Group Africa, *Algeria's Economy: The Vicious Circle of Oil and Violence*, report no. 36, October 2001.
8. Tony Hodges, *Angola: Anatomy of an Oil State*, African Issues series, International African Institute, 2004, p. 203.
9. OPEC, *Annual Statistical Bulletin 2002*.
10. EIA, *Opec Revenues Fact Sheet*.

11. George T. Abed and Hamid R. Davoodi, *Challenges of Growth and Globalization in the Middle East and North Africa*, IMF, Washington DC, 2003.

12. *Upstream*, 20 June 2003.

13. 'Oil Funds: Answer to the Paradox of Plenty', *Friends of the Earth*, November 2002.

14. 'Chad: The Tip of the Spear', *African Business*, October 2003.

15. *Upstream*, 20 June 2003.

16. Jeffrey D. Sachs and Andrew M. Warner, *Natural Resource Abundance and Economic Growth*, Harvard University Press, Cambridge MA, 1997.

17. Terry Lynn Karl, 'Reflections on the Paradox of Plenty', *Journal of International Affairs*, vol. 53, no. 1, 1999.

18. Alan Gelb and Associates, *Oil Windfalls – Blessing or Curse?*, World Bank, Washington DC, 1988, p. 89.

19. Cited in Stephen Everhart and Robert Duval-Hernandez, *Management of Oil Windfalls in Mexico*, International Finance Corporation, Washington DC, n.d.

20. Luis Giusti, 'La Apertura: The Opening of Venezuela's Oil Industry', *Journal of International Affairs*, vol. 53, no. 1, 1999.

21. *Upstream*, 2 January 2004.

22. *Daily Star*, Beirut, 29 March 2004.

23. Xavier Sala-i-Martin and Arvind Subramanian, *Addressing the Natural Resource Curse: An Illustration from Nigeria*, IMF, Washington DC, 2003.

24. Cited in Everhart and Duval-Hernandez, *Management of Oil Windfalls in Mexico*.

25. Gelb, *Oil Windfalls – Blessing or Curse?*, p. 198. Ch. 12 deals in detail with the Indonesian experience of the 1970s and 1980s.

26. Ibid., p. 158.

27. ICG Africa, *Algeria's Economy: The Vicious Circle of Oil and Violence*.

28. Ben Eifert, Alan Gelb and Nils Borje Tallroth, *The Political Economy of Fiscal Policy and Economic Management in Oil Exporting Countries*, World Bank, Washington DC, 2002.

29. United Nations, *Human Development Report 2001*, UN, Geneva, 2001, pp. 178–91. The report uses purchasing power parity figures that convert all data into a common currency and attempt to eliminate distortions resulting from differences in national prices. The procedure gives much higher income figures for developing countries that does a simple conversion into, say, dollars.

30. Eifert et al., *The Political Economy of Fiscal Policy and Economic Management in Oil Exporting Countries*.

31. Sala-i-Martin and Subramanian, *Addressing the Natural Resource Curse*.
32. Ibid.
33. Atif A. Kubursi, *Oil, Industrialisation and Development in the Arab Gulf States*, Croom Helm, Beckenham, 1984, p. 14.
34. Arabicnews.com, 2 January 2001.
35. *Daily Star*, Beirut, 13 January 2004
36. UNCTAD press releases.
37. Michael Ross, 'How Does Mineral Wealth Affect the Poor?', UCLA, 2003, www.polsci.ucla.edu/faculty/Ross/minpoor.pdf.
38. This is a simplification. In fact, the US government does own considerable subsoil assets even where surface rights are owned by private individuals.
39. Karl, 'Reflections on the Paradox of Plenty', p. 34.
40. Eifert et al., *The Political Economy of Fiscal Policy and Economic Management in Oil Exporting Countries*.
41. Petter Nore, 'Oil and the State: A Study of Nationalisation', in Petter Nore and Terisa Turner, eds, *Oil and Class Struggle*, Zed Books, London, 1980, p. 73.
42. Marshall I. Goldman, 'Russian Energy: A Blessing and a Curse', *Journal of International Affairs*, vol. 53, no. 1, 1999, p. 77.
43. 'Russian Oil and Gas: Moscow Munch', Deutsche Bank Equity Research industry update, 7 February 2003.
44. Said K. Aburish, *The Rise, Corruption and Coming Fall of the House of Saud*, Bloomsbury, London, 1995, pp. 273–302.
45. Eifert et al., *The Political Economy of Fiscal Policy and Economic Management in Oil Exporting Countries*.
46. Ehtisham Ahmad and Eric Mottu, *Oil Revenue Assignments: Country Experiences and Issues*, IMF, Washington DC, 2002.
47. *Cracks in the Marble: Turkmenistan's Failing Dictatorship*, International Crisis Group Asia report no. 44, January 2003.
48. Ike Okonta and Oronto Douglas, *Where Vulture Feast: Shell, Human Rights and Oil*, Verso, London, 2003, p. 37.
49. Terisa Turner, 'Nigeria: Imperialism, Oil Technology and the Comprador State', in Nore and Turner, eds, *Oil and Class Struggle*.
50. Phillip van Niekerk and Laura Peterson, 'Greasing the Skids of Corruption', International Consortium of Investigative Journalists, Center for Public Integrity, www.publicintegrity.com.
51. Hodges, *Angola: Anatomy of an Oil State*, p. 142.
52. Patrick Chabal and Jean-Pascal Daloz, *Africa Works: Disorder as Political Instrument*, International African Institute, Oxford, 1999, ch. 7.

53. 'Time for Transparency', *Global Witness*, Washington DC, March 2004.

54. Alain Lallemand, 'The Field Marshal', International Consortium of Investigative Journalists, Center for Public Integrity, 2002, www.publicintegrity.com.

55. The White House was later embarrassed by an investigation into allegations that the Halliburton subsidary had overcharged for fuel imported into Iraq, allegations the company vigorously rejected.

56. 'Windfalls of War: US Contractors in Iraq and Afghanistan', International Consortium of Investigative Journalists, Center for Public Integrity, 30 October 2003, www.publicintegrity.com.

57. In January 2004 Bechtel won a further contract worth $1.8 billion to repair Iraq's electricity grid and other infrastructure.

58. Jim Vallete with Steve Kretzmann and Daphne Wysham, *Crude Vision: How Oil Interests Obscured US Government Focus on Chemical Weapons Use by Saddam Hussein*, Sustainable Energy and Economy Network/Institute for Policy Studies, Washington DC, 13 August 2002.

59. Michael Ross, 'Does Oil Hinder Democracy?', *World Politics*, April 2001.

60. The measure of democracy used includes both a scale evaluating use of elections and degree of accountability and another, developed by the Freedom House organisation measuring civil liberties.

61. Paul Collier, *Economic Causes of Civil Conflict and their Implications for Policy*, World Bank, Washington DC, June 2000.

62. Paul Collier and Anke Hoeffler, *Greed and Grievance in Civil War*, World Bank, Washington DC, October 2001.

63. The following paragraphs derive largely from Michael Ross, Yale–World Bank project on the economics of political violence, *Resources and Rebellion in Aceh, Indonesia*, June 2003.

64. *Second Report on Tangguh LNG Project*, Tangguh Independent Advisory Panel, BP, London, November 2003.

65. Hodges, *Angola: Anatomy of an Oil State*, p. 159.

66. *Fuelling Poverty – Oil, War and Corruption*, Christian Aid, London, 2003, p. 29.

67. Julie Flint, writing in *Middle East International*, 7 February 2003.

68. *Middle East International*, 4 April 2003.

69. *Middle East International*, 8 March 2002.

70. 'Sudan, Oil and Human Rights', press release, Human Right Watch, 25 November 2003.

71. Ibid.

72. Press Trust of India, 14 December 2003.

73. Sudan News Agency, 15 December 2003.

74. Rainforest Action Network: background information on the U'wa people, January 2001, www.ran.org.

75. Okonta and Douglas, *Where Vulture Feast*, ch. 6.

76. Nigeria Focus, *Upstream*, 17 October 2003.

77. *Upstream*, 7 February 2003.

78. *Upstream*, 17 October 2003.

79. 'The Warri Crisis: Fuelling Violence', Human Rights Watch, December 2003.

80. Ehtisham Ahmad and Eric Mottu, *Oil Revenue Assignments: Country Experiences and Issues*, IMF, Washington DC, November 2002.

81. Ibid.

82. Sala-i-Martin and Subramanian, *Addressing the Natural Resource Curse*.

83. Charles Issawi, *An Economic History of the Middle East and North Africa*, Methuen, London, 1982, p. 205.

84. Terisa Turner, 'Iranian Oil Workers and 1978–79 Revolution', in Nore and Turner, eds, *Oil and Class Struggle*, p. 274.

85. Giusti, 'La Apertura'.

86. *Upstream*, 17 October 2003.

87. www.algeria-interface.com, 28 February 2003.

88. *Upstream*, 17 January 2003.

89. Assef Bayat, *Workers and Revolution in Iran*, Zed Books, London, 1987, p. 79.

90. Turner, 'Iranian Oil Workers and 1978–79 Revolution', p. 282.

91. *New African*, December 2002.

92. Ariel Cohen, *Iran's Claim over Caspian Sea Resources Threatens Energy Security*, Heritage Foundation, 5 September 2002, www.heritage.org/research/MiddleEast/bg1582.cfm.

93. *New York Times*, 3 September 1990.

## Chapter 3

1. Youssef M. Ibrahim, 'The 21st Century: A Time for New Oil Wars', *Daily Star*, Beirut, 23 January 2004.

2. Congressman Henry Hyde, chairman of the US House of Representatives Committee in International Relations, opening the hearing on 'Oil Diplomacy: Facts and Myths behind Foreign Oil

Dependency', 20 June 2002.

3. Congressman Ron Paul (Texas), to congressional hearing on 'Oil Diplomacy: Facts and Myths behind Foreign Oil Dependency', 20 June 2002.

4. *UK International Priorities: A Strategy for the FCO*, Foreign and Commonwealth Office, London, December 2003, p. 40.

5. In testimony to US congressional hearing on 'Oil Diplomacy: Facts and Myths behind Foreign Oil Dependency', 20 June 2002.

6. Much of the content of these paragraphs on the Cold War era is drawn from Fiona Venn, *Oil Diplomacy in the Twentieth Century*, Macmillan, London, 1986.

7. Said Aburish, *A Brutal Friendship: The West and the Arab Elite*, Gollancz, London, 1997, p. 77.

8. Ibid., p. 122.

9. PREM15/1768, National Archives, London.

10. CAB/129/173, National Archives, London.

11. Fadhil Al-Chalabi, *Opec and the International Oil Industry: A Changing Structure*, Oxford University Press, Oxford, 1980, p. 87.

12. CAB/128/53/8, National Archives, London.

13. Pierre Terzian, *OPEC: The Inside Story*, Zed Books, London, 1985, ch. 9.

14. Daniel Yergin, *The Prize: The Epic Quest for Oil, Money and Power*, Simon & Schuster, Hemel Hempstead, 1991, p. 643.

15. Oil and Security Executive Session. 14 May 2003, rapporteur's report, John F. Kennedy School of Government, Harvard University.

16. Richard Scott, *IEA: The First 20 Years*, International Energy Agency, Paris, 1994, vol. 1, p. 28.

17. Yergin, *The Prize*, p. 635.

18. Scott, *IEA: The First 20 Years*, p. 32.

19. Toby Shelley, 'Burying the Oil Demon', in Haim Bresheeth and Nira Yuval-Davis, eds, *The Gulf War and the New World Order*, Zed Books, London, 1991, p. 170.

20. Ibid., p. 171.

21. Scott, *IEA: The First 20 Years*, p. 135.

22. FT.com, 20 March 2003.

23. '1984–88 Defense Guidance', cited in Christopher Paine, 'On the Beach: The Rapid Deployment Force and the Nuclear Arms Race', *Merip Report*, January 1983, p. 11.

24. Paine, 'On the Beach, p. 11.

25. Joe Stork and Ann Lesch, 'Why War?', *Merip Report*, November–December 1990, p. 11.

26. All figures from 'US Forces Order of Battle – 13 July 2004', www.globalsecurity.org/military.

27. US congressional hearing on 'Oil Diplomacy: Facts and Myths behind Foreign Oil Dependency', 20 June 2002.

28. Ibid.

29. *National Energy Policy*, 2000, p. 8-3, www.whitehouse.gov/energy/.

30. *NATO and Caspian Security – A Mission Too Far?*, Rand Corporation/US Air Force, 2003, p. 70.

31. Dow Jones Newswires, 16 March 2004.

32. Carolyn Miles, 'The Caspian Pipeline Debate Continues: Why Not Iran?', *Journal of International Affairs*, vol. 53, no. 1, 1999, pp. 335–9.

33. US congressional hearing on 'Oil Diplomacy: Facts and Myths behind Foreign Oil Dependency', 20 June 2002.

34. Conversations with the author.

35. Fereidun Fesharaki, 'Energy and the Asian Security Nexus', *Journal of International Affairs*, vol. 53, no. 1, 1999.

36. Richard Sokolsky and Tanya Charlick-Paley, *NATO and Caspian Security – A Mission Too Far?*, RAND Corporation, Santa Monica, p. 78.

37. *Guardian*, 17 October 1998.

38. 'Energy Security and Liquefied Natural Gas', Global Energy Security Analysis, 26 September 2003, www.gasandoil.com/gesa.

39. www.shell-usgp.com/lngsasecr.asp.

40. *World Energy Outlook 2002*, International Energy Agency, Paris, 2002, p. 106.

41. Ibid., pp. 116–19.

42. International Maritime Bureau, press release, 28 January 2004.

43. *Wall Street Journal*, 11 March 2003.

44. Tim Aikens, 'Moving Security Up the Oil and Gas Agenda', *Petroleum Review*, January 2004.

45. Oil and Security Executive Session, 14 May 2003, rapporteur's report.

46. US congressional hearing on 'Oil Diplomacy: Facts and Myths behind Foreign Oil Dependency', 20 June 2002.

47. Stephen O'Sullivan, 'More Pipeline Capacity Needed to Enable Crude Exports to Expand', *Petroleum Review*, February 2004.

48. *National Energy Policy*, 2000, p. 8-3.

49. Poten & Partners, weekly market commentary, 2 January 2004.

50. Youssef Ibrahim, 'US–Mideast Oil Ties Undergo Rapid Change', *Daily Star*, Beirut, 20 January 2004.

51. 'S.14 – The Energy Policy Act of 2003', US Senate Republican Policy Committee, 7 May 2003.

52. US Department of Energy, Energy Information Administration, www.doe.eia.gov.

53. *NATO and Caspian Security – A Mission Too Far?*, pp. 76, 80.

54. Eugene Khartukov and Ellen Starostina, 'Post-Soviet Oil Exports: Are the Russians Really Coming?', *Opec Bulletin*, September/October 2003.

55. *Oil Market Report*, IEA, Paris, 11 March 2004, p. 54.

56. Dow Jones Newswires, 24 September 2003.

57. Speech, 3 October 2003, www.ExxonMobil.com.

58. Khartukov and Starostina, 'Post-Soviet Oil Exports'.

59. Reuters, 3 November 2003.

60. Analysts cited in *International Herald Tribune*, 4 November 2003.

61. For example, Bright Okogu, *The Middle East and North Africa in a Changing Oil Market*, IMF, Washington DC, 2003.

62. Joseph Romm, 'Needed – A No-regrets Energy Policy', *Bulletin of the Atomic Scientists*, July/August 1991.

63. Raad Alkadiri and Fareed Mohamedi, 'World Oil Markets and the Invasion of Iraq', *Middle East Report* 227, 2003.

64. *National Energy Policy*, 2000, p. 8-4.

65. Ashraf Faheem, 'Musical Chairs: US Policy in the Gulf', *Middle East International*, 20 August 2003.

66. Fareed Mohamedi and Raad Alkadiri, 'Washington Makes its Case for War', *Middle East Report* 224, 2002.

67. Ashraf Fahim, 'Liberating Saudi Shi'ites (and their Oil)', *Middle East International*, 2 April 2004, p. 29.

## Chapter 4

1. Pierre Terzian, *OPEC: The Inside Story*, Zed Books, London, 1985.

2. Fadhil Al-Chalabi, *Opec and the International Oil Industry: A Changing Structure*, Oxford University Press, Oxford, 1980, pp. 58–9.

3. Terzian, *OPEC: The Inside Story*, p. 264.

4. *Petroleum Intelligence Weekly*, 15 December 2003.

5. Daniel Yergin, *The Prize: The Epic Quest for Oil, Money and Power*, Simon & Schuster, Hemel Hempstead, 1991, p. 635.

6. Terzian, *OPEC: The Inside Story*, p. 207.

7. Terisa Turner, 'Nigeria: Imperialism, Oil Technology and the

Comprador State', in Petter Nore and Terisa Turner, eds, *Oil and Class Struggle*, Zed Books, London, 1980.

8. John Duke Anthony, 'The Gulf Cooperation Council: Strengths (part 2)', *Gulfwire Perspectives*, 20 February 2004.

9. 'Edward Morse, A New Political Economy of Oil?', *Journal of International Affairs*, vol. 53, no. 1, 1999, p. 14.

10. Peter Odell, *Oil and World Power*, Pelican, London, 1970, p. 25.

11. *Middle East Economic Digest*, 30 January–5 February 2004.

12. Reuters, 24 February 2004; *Upstream*, 13 February 2004.

13. Kenneth Jones, 'International Oil and Gas Agreements Not the Same as Alberta's', Diplomats International Ltd & Diplomats Overseas Ltd's *Newsletter*, April 2003.

14. *International Oil Daily*, 6 November 2003.

15. *Petroleum Review*, January 2004.

16. 'The Vital Role of Gas in a Sustainable Energy Future', speech by Malcolm Brindred, CERA conference, 11 February 2004.

17. *Upstream*, 20 February 2004.

18. Derived from BP's *Statistical Review of World Energy 2003*, p. 20.

19. This list of issues is taken from Jonathan Story, 'The Global Implications of China's Thirst for Energy', *Middle East Economic Survey*, 16 February 2004.

20. *Upstream*, 16 January 2004

21. *Financial Times*, 3 February 2004.

22. BBC News Online, 2 February 2004.

23. *China Daily*, 19 May 2003; *Upstream*, 20 February 2004.

24. Company website.

25. Company website.

26. Company website.

## Chapter 5

1. Ike Okonta and Oronto Douglas, *Where Vultures Feast*, Verso, London, 2003, ch. 4.

2. Studies commissioned by Friends of the Earth International and summarised in *Exxon's Climate Footprint*, FOE, London, January 2004.

3. *Climate Change 2001: Synthesis Report, Summary for Policymakers*, IPCC Third Assessment Report, 2001, www.grida.no/climate/ipcc_tar/wg1/.

4. G. Marland, T.A. Boden and R.G. Andres, 'Global, Regional and National Fossil Fuel $CO_2$ Emissions', in *Trends: A Compendium of Data on Global Change*, Carbon Dioxide Information Analysis Center, Oak Ridge National Laboratory, US Department of Energy, 2003, www.grida.no/climate/ipcc_tar/wg1/.

5. International Energy Agency, *Oil, Crises and Climate Challenges: 30 Years of Energy Use in IEA Countries*, IEA, Paris, 2004, p. 167.

6. Available from catherine.martin@hertscc.gov.uk.

7. *Climate Change and Its Impacts*, Hadley Centre for Climate Prediction and Research, 1998, cited in Christopher Flavin and Seth Dunn, 'A New Energy Paradigm for the 21st Century', *Journal of International Affairs*, vol. 53, no. 1, 1999, p. 172.

8. IPCC, *Climate Change 2001*, p. 9.

9. FOE, *Exxon's Climate Footprint*, p. 14.

10. Gerhard Berz and Thomas Loster, 'Climate Change – Threat and Opportunities for the Financial Sector', Munich Re website, September 2001, www.munichre.com/pdf/berz_loster_e.pdf.

11. IEA, *Oil, Crises and Climate Challenges*, p. 169.

12. Ibid., p. 170.

13. Ibid., p. 171.

14. Peter Odell, *Oil and World Power*, Pelican, London, 1970 pp. 36, 39.

15. IPCC, *Climate Change 2001*, p. 25.

16. Presentation to the Energy Institute, London, February 2004.

17. *New York Times*, 4 September 1990, cited in Jerry Taylor and Peter VanDoren, 'The Soft Case for Soft Energy', *Journal of International Affairs*, vol. 53, no. 1, 1999, p. 225.

18. FT.com, 23 December 2003.

19. *The Observer*, 22 February 2004.

20. US President Jimmy Carter, *1981 State of the Union Message*, London.

21. International Energy Agency, *World Energy Outlook 2002*, IEA, Paris, 2002, pp. 58–60.

22. UN Commission on Trade and Development website, www.unctad.org/infocomm.

23. Leonidas Barrow, 'Domestic Natural Gas: The Coming Methane Economy', *Geotimes*, November 2002.

24. *Upstream*, 19 March 2004.

25. Gordon Cope, 'Small Production Heralds Big Future', *Petroleum Review*, March 2004.

26. Company website www.suncor.com.

27. IEA, *Oil, Crises and Climate Challenges*, p. 101.
28. Government of Alberta website, www.energy.gov.ab.ca/com.
29. *Upstream*, 12 March 2004.
30. For further information on gas-to-liquids technology and prospects see *Fundamentals of Gas to Liquids*, Petroleum Economist Ltd, London, in association with Sasol-Chevron. Prospects for the technology in the Middle East are discussed in Paul McDonald, 'Middle East Looks Downstream for New Gas Prospects', *Petroleum Review*, December 2003.
31. Merrill Lynch New Energy Technology plc, *Annual Report*, 31 October 2003, p. 6.
32. Joe Barnes, Amy Jaffe and Edward Morse, 'The New Geopolitics of Oil', *The National Interest*, Energy Supplement, Winter 2003/04.
33. 'Moving to a Hydrogen Economy: Dreams and Realities', research note by the secretariat of the Standing Group on Long-term Co-operation, IEA, Paris, 30 January 2003, p. 5.
34. Ibid., p. 6.
35. IEA, *World Energy Outlook 2002*, p. 338.

## Conclusion

1. Speech of 27 April 2004, reproduced by Saudi–US Relations Information Service, 11 May 2004, www.Saudi-US-Relations.org.
2. Energy Information Administration, *International Energy Outlook*, 2004, Highlights, p. 3.
3. International Energy Agency, *World Energy Outlook 2002*, IEA, Paris, 2002, p. 91.
4. *The Impact of Higher Oil Price on the World Economy*, IEA Standing Group on Long-Term Cooperation, report summary, Paris, 2003.
5. IEA, *World Energy Outlook 2002*, pp. 73–8.
6. 'The Impact of Higher Oil Price on the Global Economy', IMF Research Department, December 2000, www.imf.org/external/pubs/ft/oil/2000/.
7. Reuters, 19 April 2004.
8. Henry Azzam, 'Export-driven Growth in Middle East Likely to Continue in 2004', *Daily Star*, Beirut, 27 April 2004.
9. 'OPEC Revenues Fact Sheet', Energy Information Administration, January 2004, www.eia.doe.gov.
10. 'Will Russia Double GDP without High Oil Prices?', August 2003,

www.worldbank.org.ru/ECA/Russia.nsf.

11. 'Energy Price Impacts on the US Economy, Energy Information Administration, April 2001, available on www.eia.doe.gov
12. Press release, IEA, 1 April 2004.
13. 'Who Gets What from Imported Oil', OPEC, available on www. opec.org.
14. ICEM press release, 30 June 2004.
15. *Financial Times*, 29 October 2003.
16. *Upstream*, 19 September 2003.
17. 'Time for Transparency: Coming Clean on Oil, Mining and Gas Revenues', *Global Witness*, Washington DC, March 2004, pp. 53–64.
18. *Financial Times*, 20 April 2004; *Upstream*, 13 April 2004.

# Index

A BRAVE NEW SERIES

# Global Issues
# in a Changing World

This new series of short, accessible think-pieces deals with leading
global issues of relevance to humanity today. Intended for the
enquiring reader and social activists in the North and the South,
as well as students, the books explain what is at stake and question
conventional ideas and policies. Drawn from many different parts of
the world, the series' authors pay particular attention to the needs
and interests of ordinary people, whether living in the rich industrial
or the developing countries. They all share a common objective – to
help stimulate new thinking and social action in the opening years
of the new century.

Global Issues in a Changing World is a joint initiative by Zed
Books in collaboration with a number of partner publishers and non-
governmental organizations around the world. By working together,
we intend to maximize the relevance and availability of the books
published in the series.


## Participating NGOs

Both ENDS, Amsterdam
Catholic Institute for International Relations, London
Corner House, Sturminster Newton
Council on International and Public Affairs, New York
Dag Hammarskjöld Foundation, Uppsala
Development GAP, Washington DC
Focus on the Global South, Bangkok
IBON, Manila
Inter Pares, Ottawa
Public Interest Research Centre, Delhi
Third World Network, Penang
Third World Network–Africa, Accra
World Development Movement, London

# About this series

'Communities in the South are facing great difficulties in coping with global trends. I hope this brave new series will throw much needed light on the issues ahead and help us choose the right options.'

MARTIN KHOR, *Director,*
*Third World Network, Penang*

'There is no more important campaign than our struggle to bring the global economy under democratic control. But the issues are fearsomely complex. This Global Issues series is a valuable resource for the committed campaigner and the educated citizen.'

BARRY COATES, *Director,*
*World Development Movement (WDM)*

'Zed Books has long provided an inspiring list about the issues that touch and change people's lives. The Global Issues series is another dimension of Zed's fine record, allowing access to a range of subjects and authors that, to my knowledge, very few publishers have tried. I strongly recommend these new, powerful titles and this exciting series.'

JOHN PILGER, *author*

'We are all part of a generation that actually has the means to eliminate extreme poverty world-wide. Our task is to harness the forces of globalization for the benefit of working people, their families and their communities – that is our collective duty. The Global Issues series makes a powerful contribution to the global campaign for justice, sustainable and equitable development, and peaceful progress.'

GLENYS KINNOCK, *MEP*

# The Global Issues series

### *Already available*

Peggy Antrobus, *The International Women's Movement: Issues and Strategies*

Walden Bello, *Deglobalization: Ideas for a New World Economy*

Robert Ali Brac de la Perrière and Franck Seuret, *Brave New Seeds: The Threat of GM Crops to Farmers*

Greg Buckman, *Globalization: Tame it or Scrap It? Mapping the Alternatives of the Anti-Globalization Movement*

Ha-Joon Chang and Ilene Grabel, *Reclaiming Development: An Alternative Economic Policy Handbook*

Oswaldo de Rivero, *The Myth of Development: The Non-viable Economies of the 21st Century*

Graham Dunkley, *Free Trade: Myth, Reality and Alternatives*

Joyeeta Gupta, *Our Simmering Planet: What to Do about Global Warming?*

Nicholas Guyatt, *Another American Century? The United States and the World since 9/11*

Martin Khor, *Rethinking Globalization: Critical Issues and Policy Choices*

John Madeley, *Food for All: The Need for a New Agriculture*

John Madeley, *Hungry for Trade: How the Poor Pay for Free Trade*

A.G. Noorani, *Islam and Jihad: Prejudice versus Reality*

Riccardo Petrella, *The Water Manifesto: Arguments for a World Water Contract*

Peter Robbins, *Stolen Fruit: The Tropical Commodities Disaster*

Toby Shelley, *Oil and Gas: What Future? What Consequences?*

Vandana Shiva, *Protect or Plunder? Understanding Intellectual Property Rights*

Harry Shutt, *A New Democracy: Alternatives to a Bankrupt World Order*

Kavaljit Singh, *The Myth of Globalization: Ten Questions Everyone Asks*

David Sogge, *Give and Take: What's the Matter with Foreign Aid?*

Paul Todd and Jonathan Bloch, *Global Intelligence: The World's Secret Services Today*

For full details of this list and Zed's other subject and general catalogues, please write to: The Marketing Department, Zed Books, 7 Cynthia Street, London NI 9JF, UK or email Sales@zedbooks.demon.co.uk

Visit our website at: www.zedbooks.co.uk

# Participating organizations

**Both ENDS**  A service and advocacy organization which collaborates with environment and indigenous organizations, both in the South and in the North, with the aim of helping to create and sustain a vigilant and effective environmental movement.

Nieuwe Keizersgracht 45, 1018 VC Amsterdam, The Netherlands
Phone: +31 20 623 0823    Fax: +31 20 620 8049
Email: info@bothends.org    Website: www.bothends.org

**Catholic Institute for International Relations (CIIR)**  CIIR aims to contribute to the eradication of poverty through a programme that combines advocacy at national and international level with community-based development.

Unit 3, Canonbury Yard, 190a New North Road, London N1 7BJ, UK
Phone +44 (0)20 7354 0883    Fax +44 (0)20 7359 0017
Email: ciir@ciir.org    Website: www.ciir.org

**Corner House**  The Corner House is a UK-based research and solidarity group working on social and environmental justice issues in North and South.

PO Box 3137, Station Road, Sturminster Newton, Dorset DT10 1YJ, UK
Tel.: +44 (0)1258 473795    Fax: +44 (0)1258 473748
Email: cornerhouse@gn.apc.org  Website: www.cornerhouse.icaap.org

**Council on International and Public Affairs (CIPA)**  CIPA is a human rights research, education and advocacy group, with a particular focus on economic and social rights in the USA and elsewhere around the world. Emphasis in recent years has been given to resistance to corporate domination.

777 United Nations Plaza, Suite 3C, New York, NY 10017, USA
Tel. +1 212 972 9877    Fax +1 212 972 9878
Email: cipany@igc.org    Website: www.cipa-apex.org

**Dag Hammarskjöld Foundation**  The Dag Hammarskjöld Foundation, established 1962, organises seminars and workshops on social, economic and cultural issues facing developing countries with a particular focus on alternative and innovative solutions. Results are published in its journal *Develpment Dialogue*.

Övre Slottsgatan 2, 753 10 Uppsala, Sweden.
Tel.: +46 18 102772    Fax: +46 18 122072
Email: secretariat@dhf.uu.se    Website: www.dhf.uu.se

**Development GAP** The Development Group for Alternative Policies is a Non-Profit Development Resource Organization working with popular organizations in the South and their Northern partners in support of a development that is truly sustainable and that advances social justice.

927 15th Street NW, 4th Floor, Washington, DC, 20005, USA
Tel.: +1 202 898 1566    Fax: +1 202 898 1612
E-mail: dgap@igc.org    Website: www.developmentgap.org

**Focus on the Global South** Focus is dedicated to regional and global policy analysis and advocacy work. It works to strengthen the capacity of organizations of the poor and marginalized people of the South and to better analyse and understand the impacts of the globalization process on their daily lives.

C/o CUSRI, Chulalongkorn University, Bangkok 10330, Thailand
Tel.: +66 2 218 7363 Fax: +66 2 255 9976
Email: Admin@focusweb.org    Website: www.focusweb.org

**IBON** IBON Foundation is a research, education and information institution that provides publications and services on socio-economic issues as support to advocacy in the Philippines and abroad. Through its research and databank, formal and non-formal education programmes, media work and international networking, IBON aims to build the capacity of both Philippine and international organizations.

Room 303 SCC Bldg, 4427 Int. Old Sta. Mesa, Manila 1008, Philippines
Phone +632 7132729    Fax +632 7160108
Email: editors@ibon.org    Website: www.ibon.org

**Inter Pares** Inter Pares, a Canadian social justice organization, has been active since 1975 in building relationships with Third World development groups and providing support for community-based development programmes. Inter Pares is also involved in education and advocacy in Canada, promoting understanding about the causes, effects and solutions to poverty.

221 Laurier Avenue East, Ottawa, Ontario, KIN 6PI Canada
Phone +1 613 563 4801    Fax +1 613 594 4704
Email: info@interpares.ca    Website: www.interpares.ca

**Public Interest Research Centre** PIRC is a research and campaigning group based in Delhi which seeks to serve the information needs of activists and organizations working on macro-economic issues concerning finance, trade and development.

142 Maitri Apartments, Plot No. 28, Patparganj, Delhi 110092, India
Phone: +91 11 2221081/2432054    Fax: +91 11 2224233
Email: kaval@nde.vsnl.net.in

**Third World Network**  TWN is an international network of groups and individuals involved in efforts to bring about a greater articulation of the needs and rights of peoples in the Third World; a fair distribution of the world's resources; and forms of development which are ecologically sustainable and fulfil human needs. Its international secretariat is based in Penang, Malaysia.

121-S Jalan Utama, 10450 Penang, Malaysia
Tel.: +60 4 226 6159     Fax: +60 4 226 4505
Email: twnet@po.jaring.my     Website: www.twnside.org.sg

**Third World Network–Africa**  TWN–Africa is engaged in research and advocacy on economic, environmental and gender issues. In relation to its current particular interest in globalization and Africa, its work focuses on trade and investment, the extractive sectors and gender and economic reform.

2 Ollenu Street, East Legon, PO Box AN19452, Accra-North, Ghana.
Tel.: +233 21 511189/503669/500419     Fax: +233 21 511188
Email: twnafrica@ghana.com

**World Development Movement (WDM)**  The World Development Movement campaigns to tackle the causes of poverty and injustice. It is a democratic membership movement that works with partners in the South to cancel unpayable debt and break the ties of IMF conditionality, for fairer trade and investment rules, and for strong international rules on multinationals.

25 Beehive Place, London SW9 7QR, UK
Tel.: +44 (0)20 7737 6215     Fax: +44 (0)20 7274 8232
Email: wdm@wdm.org.uk     Website: www.wdm.org.uk

# This book is also available in the following countries

CARIBBEAN

Arawak Publications
17 Kensington Crescent
Apt 5
Kingston 5, Jamaica
Tel: 876 960 7538
Fax: 876 960 9219

EGYPT

MERIC
(Middle East Readers'
Information Center)
2 Bahgat Ali Street,
Tower D/Apt. 24
Zamalek, Cairo
Tel: 20 2 735 3818/3824
Fax: 20 2 736 9355

FIJI

University Book Centre,
University of South Pacific
Suva
Tel: 679 313 900
Fax: 679 303 265

GHANA

Readwide Books Ltd
12 Ablade Road
Kanda Estates, Kanda
Accra, Ghana
Tel: 233 244 630 805
Tel: 233 208 180 310

GUYANA

Austin's Book Services
190 Church St
Cummingsburg
Georgetown
Tel: 592 227 7395
Fax: 592 227 7396

IRAN

Book City
743 North Hafez Avenue
15977 Tehran
Tel: 98 21 889 7875
Fax: 98 21 889 7785
bookcity@neda.net

MAURITIUS

Editions Le Printemps
4 Club Rd, Vacoas

MOZAMBIQUE

Sul Sensações
PO Box 2242, Maputo
Tel: 258 1 421974
Fax: 258 1 423414

NAMIBIA

Book Den
PO Box 3469
Shop 4
Frans Indongo Gardens
Windhoek
Tel: 264 61 239976
Fax: 264 61 234248

NEPAL

Everest Media Services,
GPO Box 5443
Dillibazar
Putalisadak Chowk
Kathmandu
Tel: 977 1 416026
Fax: 977 1 250176

NIGERIA

Mosuro Publishers
52 Magazine Road
Jericho
Ibadan
Tel: 234 2 241 3375
Fax: 234 2 241 3374

PAKISTAN

Vanguard Books
45 The Mall, Lahore
Tel: 92 42 735 5079
Fax: 92 42 735 5197

PAPUA NEW GUINEA

Unisearch PNG Pty Ltd
Box 320, University
National Capital District
Tel: 675 326 0130
Fax: 675 326 0127

RWANDA

Librairie Ikirezi
PO Box 443
Kigali
Tel/Fax: 250 71314

SUDAN

The Nile Bookshop
New Extension Street 41
PO Box 8036
Khartoum
Tel: 249 11 463 749

UGANDA

Aristoc Booklex Ltd
PO Box 5130,
Kampala Road
Diamond Trust Building
Kampala
Tel/Fax: 256 41 254867

ZAMBIA

UNZA Press
PO Box 32379
Lusaka
Tel: 260 1 290409
Fax: 260 1 253952

ZIMBABWE

Weaver Press
PO Box A1922
Avondale, Harare
Tel: 263 4 308330
Fax: 263 4 339645